THE   BOOK   OF

FIRST
COURSES

T H E   B O O K   O F

FIRST COURSES

LESLEY MACKLEY

Photographed by
SIMON BUTCHER

HPBooks

ANOTHER BEST SELLING VOLUME FROM HP BOOKS

HPBooks
Published by The Berkley Publishing Group
200 Madison Avenue
New York, NY 10016

9 8 7 6 5 4 3 2 1

ISBN 1-55788-221-5

First Edition ~ December 1995

By arrangement with Salamander Books Ltd.

Food Stylist: Jane Charlton
Printed in Belgium by Proost International Book Production

CONTENTS

INTRODUCTION

When planning a dinner party, it's all too easy to devote your time and effort to the main course, overlooking the scores of delicious ways to begin a meal. Choosing the right starter will turn any get-together into a special occasion. With *The Book of First Courses* handy you'll never be short of inspiration; it features a tempting and varied array of dishes inspired by cuisines from all over the world. There are over one hundred recipes, including an impressive Fish and Watercress Terrine, crispy Shrimp and Feta Bundles, a refreshing Chilled Melon Soup and spicy Cheesy Quesadillas. And if you're looking for original ideas for meals, you'll find the recipes offer so much more than simply tasty appetizers. On their own, many make satisfying lunch dishes or snacks, or you can borrow an idea popular in Greece and Spain and serve your guests a whole selection of tempting small dishes for an unusual light meal that everyone will enjoy.

PLANNING A MENU

In many ways, the first course is the most important. The starter sets the tone for the whole meal and should whet the appetite for the courses to follow. It should not overpower the main course, but build up to it as temptingly as possible. Choose your starter with a little care and it will play a large part in the success of your meal.

CHOOSING YOUR STARTER

If organising a dinner party or even just an informal family meal, it is worth taking time to plan the menu carefully, to ensure that there is a good balance of flavors, textures and colors throughout the meal. Since the appetite is stimulated by the sight of an attractively presented dish, the appearance of the first course is particularly important. It is essential to arrange the food carefully and to think of ways to garnish it for extra effect. Even something as simple as croûtons in a bowl of soup or chopped fresh herbs scattered over a salad can make all the difference.

Individual dishes look particularly attractive, so whenever possible serve your guests single portions, such as mousses or soufflés made in ramekins

Below, left to right: Prosciutto Baskets; Baked Eggplant Layers; Chicken & Crab Rolls; Spinach Salad; Pears with Stilton Sauce; Shrimp & Feta Purses.

rather than one large dish, or individual tartlets instead of slices from a single large tart. This also makes serving easier, as the portions can be placed directly on each plate.

When planning your menu it is also important to consider the appearance of the dishes. Avoid serving a meal where all the courses are similar in color, such as chicken liver pâté followed by a meat casserole and then a chocolate mousse. In the same way, the texture of the dishes should be as varied as possible. Nobody would enjoy a meal where every dish was smothered in sauce any more than if everything was dry and crisp. It is quite simple to add texture to a dish - serve crusty bread with a smooth terrine, for example, or add toasted nuts to a salad.

BALANCED MEALS

Most people today are very health conscious and would not appreciate a meal consisting of several rich and filling dishes. A substantial main course should be preceded by a light and refreshing starter such as a vegetable or salad dish. A richer first course, like pasta or a cheese dish, should be followed by a light fish, chicken or vegetable dish. Bear in mind that most people are cutting down on their meat consumption, so avoid serving large quantities of meat in both the first and second courses.

TIMING YOUR MEAL

One of the secrets of a successful dinner party is a relaxed host or hostess who has time to spend with the guests. So plan a menu that avoids more than one dish requiring last minute attention. Warm salads, soufflés and accompaniments such as hollandaise sauce are best for occasions where the main course is ready to serve well in advance, and recipes such as tempura, which must be served as soon as it is cooked, are most suitable for informal gatherings where the guests are sitting at the kitchen table ready to eat the food while it is still hot. If you have chosen a main course that requires last minute attention, there are many starters which can be arranged on individual plates and laid on the table well before the start of the meal.

SIMPLE STARTERS

Some of the best starters are also the simplest. These are dishes which rely less on the skill of the cook than on the ability to shop for fresh, high quality ingredients. A simple selection of salami from a good delicatessen accompanied by a few olives and a loaf of fresh bread is all you need for a delicious Mediterranean-style starter. Or serve an attractively arranged platter of smoked fish and shellfish, or a selection of dips with crisp, fresh vegetables. Fresh asparagus served with melted butter is all the more delicious because its season is short,

Above, far left to right: Leek & Lemon Grass Soup; Carpaccio; Seafood Diamonds; Artichokes with Aïoli; Mexican Seviche; Asparagus Tartlets.

and in the summer, when tomatoes are at their sweetest, a simple salad of sliced tomatoes, a few fresh herbs and olive oil cannot be bettered. Avocado with vinaigrette requires a minimum of preparation, but as long as it is made with the best olive oil and vinegar or lemon juice, it will be appreciated by everyone. For a dramatic special touch, slice the avocados and fan them out on individual plates.

VERSATILE DISHES

In some countries, the first course is more of a meal in itself, such as the *tapas* of Spain, the *antipasti* of Italy and the *meze* of Greece. It is fun to borrow this idea and make a variety of different starters to set out in a tempting array so your guests can help themselves to whatever they fancy.

Most recipes for starters can make a light lunch or supper dish. Similarly, there are many main course dishes which, when served in smaller quantities, are perfect for starters. Pasta, traditionally served as a starter in Italy, and fish dishes are particularly suitable for main courses, as are quiches and mousses.

Whatever the occasion, simply devote a little time and attention to your menu planning and your starters will always be successful.

MUSHROOM SOUP

1 oz. dried cepes (porcini mushrooms)
2 tablespoons olive oil
1 tablespoon butter
4 shallots, chopped
2 garlic cloves, crushed
1 lb. brown mushrooms, sliced
3-3/4 cups chicken stock
Grated zest of 1 lemon
2 tablespoons chopped fresh tarragon
2/3 cup whipping cream
Salt and freshly ground pepper
Tarragon sprigs, to garnish
CROÛTONS:
3 slices white bread, crusts removed
2 tablespoons sunflower oil

Put cepes in a bowl and cover with lukewarm water. Let soak 30 minutes. Heat oil and butter in a large saucepan, add shallots and garlic and cook, stirring occasionally, 5 minutes or until soft. Add brown mushrooms and cook, stirring occasionally, 5 minutes. Drain cepes, reserving soaking liquid. Add cepes, stock and lemon zest to pan. Bring to a boil, reduce heat, cover and simmer 30 to 40 minutes or until cepes are tender.

Meanwhile, make croûtons. Cut bread into small cubes. Heat oil in a skillet, add bread and fry, turning, until golden and crisp. Remove with a slotted spoon and drain on paper towels. Purée soup in a blender or food processor. Return soup to rinsed-out pan and stir in enough reserved soaking liquid to give desired consistency. Add tarragon, cream, salt and pepper and reheat gently without boiling. Garnish with croûtons and tarragon sprigs and serve.

Makes 6 servings.

—— CHILLED AVOCADO SOUP ——

2 ripe avocados
2/3 cup regular plain yogurt
3-3/4 cups chicken stock
Grated zest of 1 lime
Salt and freshly ground pepper
2 tablespoons chopped fresh chives

Halve avocados lengthwise and remove pits. Using a teaspoon, scoop out avocado flesh, taking care to scrape away dark green flesh closest to skin.

Put avocado into a blender or food processor. Add yogurt and one-third of chicken stock and purée until smooth. Stir in remaining stock, lime zest, salt and pepper.

Pour into a bowl, cover and refrigerate 2 hours. Serve in chilled bowls, garnished with chives.

Makes 6 servings.

——SUGAR SNAP PEA SOUP——

1 bunch green onions
1/4 cup butter
1 lb. sugar snap peas
6 oz. potatoes, diced
4-1/2 cups vegetable stock
2/3 cup half-and-half
2 tablespoons chopped fresh tarragon
Salt and freshly ground pepper
Shredded green onion, to garnish

Chop green onions. Melt butter in a large saucepan over medium heat. Add chopped green onions and peas and cook, stirring, 2 minutes or until beginning to soften.

Add potatoes and stock. Bring to a boil, reduce heat, cover and simmer 20 minutes or until vegetables are tender. Purée soup in a blender or food processor. Press through a strainer and return to rinsed-out pan.

Stir half-and-half into soup. Add tarragon, season with salt and pepper and reheat gently without boiling. Garnish with shredded green onion and serve.

Makes 6 servings.

- BLUE CHEESE & BROCCOLI SOUP -

6 oz. potatoes
2 tablespoons butter
1 onion, finely chopped
4-1/2 cups chicken stock
12 oz. broccoli
Salt and freshly ground pepper
4 oz. blue cheese
GARLIC CROÛTONS:
2 slices white bread, crusts removed
2 tablespoons sunflower oil
1 tablespoon butter
1 garlic clove, finely chopped

Peel potatoes and cut into 1-inch cubes.

Melt butter in a large saucepan over medium heat. Add onion and cook, stirring occasionally, 5 minutes or until soft. Add stock and potatoes, bring to a boil, reduce heat, cover and simmer 10 minutes. Cut broccoli into flowerets and add to pan. Return to a boil, reduce heat, cover and simmer 10 minutes or until vegetables are tender.

Meanwhile, make croûtons. Cut bread into shapes with a pastry cutter. Heat oil, butter and garlic in a skillet and fry bread shapes on both sides until golden and crisp. Remove with a slotted spoon and drain on paper towels. Purée soup in a blender or food processor. Return to rinsed-out pan, add salt and pepper, then crumble in cheese. Reheat gently without boiling, until cheese has melted. Garnish with croûtons and serve.

Makes 6 servings.

GREEN GAZPACHO

1 fennel bulb
1 green bell pepper, quartered
2 stalks celery, sliced
4 green onions, sliced
1/2 cucumber, peeled, seeded and diced
1 garlic clove, chopped
1/4 cup olive oil
Juice of 1/2 lemon
Salt and freshly ground pepper
Cucumber ribbons, to garnish

Bring a saucepan of water to a boil. Trim fennel, cut lengthwise into quarters and slice.

Put fennel into boiling water and cook 3 minutes. Drain, reserving water. Rinse fennel in cold water and leave to drain. Put bell pepper, celery, green onions, cucumber, garlic and fennel into a blender or food processor and process until finely chopped, but retaining a little texture.

Pour into a large bowl, stir in olive oil and lemon juice and season with salt and pepper. Stir in 1-1/4 cups reserved fennel cooking water, adding more water if necessary to give desired consistency. Cover and refrigerate at least 2 hours. Serve in chilled bowls, garnished with cucumber ribbons.

Makes 4 to 6 servings.

SOUPE AU PISTOU

1/2 cup dried haricot beans, soaked overnight and
    drained
1/4 cup olive oil
2 leeks, white parts only, chopped
1 carrot, diced
2 stalks celery, thinly sliced
4-1/4 cups hot water
4 oz. shelled broad beans or lima beans (about 2/3
    cup)
6 oz. small green beans, cut into 1-inch lengths
    (about 1-1/3 cups)
2 zucchini, diced
3 tomatoes, peeled and coarsely chopped
Salt and freshly ground pepper
3 tablespoons pesto
Parmesan shavings, to garnish

Put haricot beans into a large saucepan, cover
with cold water and bring to a boil. Boil
rapidly 10 minutes, cover and simmer 30
minutes. Drain. Heat oil in a large saucepan.
Add leeks, carrot and celery and cook,
stirring occasionally, 5 minutes or until
beginning to soften.

Add hot water and haricot beans to pan.
Bring to a boil, cover and cook over low heat
30 to 40 minutes or until beans are tender.
Add broad beans, green beans, zucchini and
tomatoes and cook 10 minutes or until all
vegetables are tender. Season with salt and
pepper and stir in pesto. Serve hot, garnished
with shavings of Parmesan cheese.

Makes 6 to 8 servings.

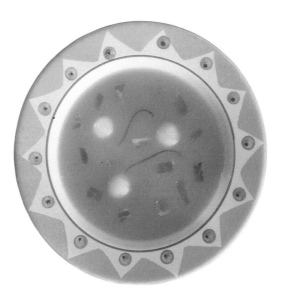

– CHILLED MELON & HAM SOUP –

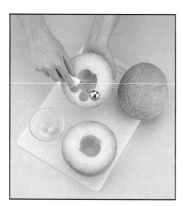

2 ripe cantaloupe or Galia melons
8 oz. cucumber
Finely pared zest of 1 lime
2 tablespoons sugar
1-1/4 cups water
Salt and freshly ground pepper
4 oz. prosciutto

Halve melons and remove seeds. Scoop out a few small balls of melon with a melon baller, or scoop out 2 tablespoons melon flesh and cut into small dice. Set aside.

Remove remaining melon flesh with a spoon and coarsely chop. Put melon into a saucepan. Peel cucumber, halve lengthwise and remove seeds. Coarsely chop flesh and add to saucepan. Add lime zest, sugar and water. Heat, stirring, until sugar has dissolved. Bring to a boil, reduce heat, cover and simmer 10 minutes.

Purée soup in a blender or food processor. Press through a strainer into a bowl. Season with salt and pepper. Let cool, cover and refrigerate at least 2 hours. Trim fat from prosciutto. Finely chop prosciutto and stir into soup with reserved pieces of melon. Serve in chilled bowls.

Makes 6 servings.

—ROASTED BELL PEPPER SOUP—

6 large tomatoes
1 garlic clove, chopped
1/3 cup olive oil
Salt and freshly ground pepper
4 red bell peppers, quartered
1 onion, finely chopped
6 oz. potatoes, cut into 3/4-inch cubes
3-3/4 cups water
Shredded basil leaves, to garnish
BASIL PUREE:
1 small bunch of basil
2 tablespoons olive oil
1 teaspoon lemon juice

Preheat oven to 350F (180C). Oil two roasting pans. Cut tomatoes in half.

Place tomatoes, cut side up, in one of the roasting pans. Scatter garlic and drizzle 2 tablespoons of the oil over tomatoes. Season with salt and pepper. Place bell peppers in the other pan. Drizzle with 2 tablespoons of the oil. Put tomatoes and bell peppers in oven and cook tomatoes 45 to 60 minutes or until beginning to blacken around edges. Cook bell peppers, turning occasionally, until their skins are charred and blistered. Put bell peppers into a plastic bag and leave until cool enough to handle. Peel bell peppers and coarsely chop.

Heat remaining oil in a large saucepan. Add onion and cook, stirring occasionally, 5 minutes or until soft. Add potatoes, bell peppers and water. Cover and simmer 20 minutes. Transfer to a blender or food processor, add tomatoes and purée. Press through a strainer, return to rinsed-out pan and heat through. Season. Pound basil leaves with a large pinch of salt. Stir in oil and lemon juice. Drizzle basil purée on to soup, garnish and serve.

Makes 6 servings.

SPICED LENTIL SOUP

2 onions
2 garlic cloves
4 tomatoes
1/2 teaspoon ground turmeric
1 teaspoon ground cumin
6 cardamom pods
1/2 cinnamon stick
1-1/4 cups red lentils
3-3/4 cups water
1 (14-oz.) can coconut milk
1 tablespoon lemon juice
Salt and freshly ground pepper
Cumin seeds, to garnish

Finely chop onions and garlic cloves. Coarsely chop tomatoes.

Put onions, garlic, tomatoes, turmeric, cumin, cardamom pods, cinnamon stick, lentils and water into a large saucepan. Bring to a boil, reduce heat, cover and simmer 20 minutes, or until lentils are soft.

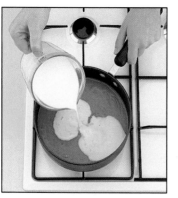

Remove cardamom pods and cinnamon stick, then purée lentil mixture in a blender or food processor. Press soup through a strainer and return to rinsed-out pan. Reserve a little coconut milk for garnish and add remainder to pan with lemon juice, salt and pepper. Reheat gently without boiling. Swirl in reserved coconut milk, garnish with cumin seeds and serve.

Makes 6 servings.

— BUTTERNUT SQUASH SOUP —

1 butternut squash
2 apples
2 tablespoons butter
1 onion, finely chopped
1 or 2 teaspoons curry powder
2-1/2 cups chicken or vegetable stock
1 teaspoon chopped fresh sage
2/3 cup apple juice
Salt and freshly ground pepper
Curry powder and sage leaves, to garnish
CURRIED HORSERADISH CREAM:
1/4 cup whipping cream
2 teaspoons prepared horseradish
1/2 teaspoon curry powder

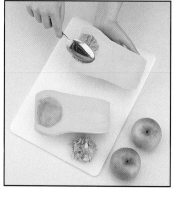

Peel squash, remove seeds and chop flesh.

Peel, core and chop apples. Melt butter in a large saucepan. Add onion and cook, stirring occasionally, 5 minutes or until soft. Add curry powder and cook, stirring constantly, 2 minutes. Add stock, squash, apples and sage. Bring to a boil, reduce heat, cover and simmer 20 minutes or until squash and apples are soft.

Meanwhile, make curried horseradish cream. In a bowl, whip cream until stiff. Stir in horseradish and curry powder. Cover and refrigerate until required. Purée soup in a blender or food processor. Return to rinsed-out pan, add apple juice, salt and pepper and reheat gently without boiling. Top each serving with a spoonful of horseradish cream, sprinkle with curry powder, garnish with sage leaves and serve.

Makes 6 servings.

— LEEK & LEMON GRASS SOUP —

1 onion
2 large leeks
6 oz. potatoes
3 tablespoons butter
3-3/4 cups chicken stock
3 stalks lemon grass
Salt and freshly ground pepper
1-1/4 cups milk
Crème fraîche and chopped fresh cilantro, to
  garnish

Finely chop onion. Trim leeks, wash, and finely slice. Peel potatoes and cut into 3/4-inch cubes.

Melt butter in a large saucepan. Add onion and leeks and stir well to coat with butter. Cover pan and cook over low heat, stirring occasionally, 10 minutes. Add stock and potatoes. Lightly crush lemon grass and add to pan. Bring to a boil, reduce heat, cover and simmer 20 minutes or until potatoes are tender. Remove lemon grass and discard. Purée soup in a blender or food processor.

Return soup to rinsed-out pan. Add salt and pepper and stir in milk. Reheat gently without boiling. Top each serving with a spoonful of crème fraîche, garnish with chopped cilantro and serve.

Makes 6 servings.

THAI COCONUT SOUP

1 small bunch cilantro
1-3/4 cups chicken stock
1-inch piece ginger root, peeled and finely chopped
1 garlic clove, crushed
6 green onions, chopped
2 stalks lemon grass, chopped
1 fresh red chile, cored, seeded and chopped
4 kaffir lime leaves (optional)
1 (14-oz.) can coconut milk
Juice of 1 lime
1 tablespoon Thai fish sauce
Cilantro leaves, to garnish

Separate cilantro stalks from leaves. Coarsely chop stalks and finely chop leaves.

Put chicken stock into a large saucepan. Add cilantro stalks, ginger root, garlic, half the green onions, lemon grass, chile and lime leaves, if using. Bring to a boil, reduce heat, cover and simmer 30 minutes. Strain soup into a clean pan. Add coconut milk, lime juice and fish sauce.

Stir in remaining green onions. Bring to a boil, reduce heat and simmer 5 minutes. Stir in chopped cilantro leaves, garnish with whole cilantro leaves and serve.

Makes 6 servings.

──── TUSCAN BEAN SOUP ────

3/4 cup dried red kidney beans, soaked overnight and drained
3/4 cup dried haricot beans, soaked overnight and drained
2 tablespoons olive oil
1 large onion, finely chopped
2 garlic cloves, crushed
4 stalks celery, thinly sliced
1 (14-oz.) can crushed tomatoes
3-3/4 cups vegetable or ham stock
Salt and freshly ground pepper
1 tablespoon chopped fresh marjoram
Marjoram sprigs, to garnish

Put kidney and haricot beans in a large saucepan and cover with cold water.

Bring to a boil and boil rapidly 10 minutes. Cover and simmer 45 minutes, or until beans are tender. Drain beans, reserving cooking liquid. Put half the beans and some of the cooking liquid in a blender or food processor and purée until smooth.

Heat oil in a large saucepan. Add onion, garlic and celery and cook over low heat, stirring occasionally, 5 minutes or until soft. Stir in bean purée, tomatoes, stock, and remaining beans. Bring to a boil, reduce heat, cover and simmer 30 minutes. Add enough reserved cooking liquid, if necessary, to give desired consistency. Season with salt and pepper. Stir in marjoram, garnish with marjoram sprigs and serve.

Makes 6 servings.

── FENNEL & PEAR SOUP ──

2 fennel bulbs
2 tablespoons butter
3 ripe pears
3-3/4 cups chicken or vegetable stock
2/3 cup crème fraîche or thick sour cream
Salt and freshly ground pepper
Crème fraîche or thick sour cream and chopped
    fennel leaves, to garnish

Trim fennel, cut lengthwise into quarters and coarsely chop. Melt butter in a saucepan, add fennel and cook 5 minutes, stirring occasionally, until beginning to soften.

Peel pears, cut into quarters and remove cores. Coarsely chop pears and add to pan. Stir in stock. Bring to a boil, reduce heat, cover and simmer 15 minutes or until fennel and pears are tender.

Purée soup in a blender or food processor. Return to rinsed-out pan and stir in crème fraîche or sour cream, salt and pepper. Refrigerate at least 2 hours. Serve in chilled bowls, or reheat and serve hot. Garnish with a swirl of crème fraîche or sour cream and fennel leaves.

Makes 6 servings.

—FRENCH-STYLE FISH SOUP—

2 lbs. mixed fish and shellfish, including white fish
  fillets, mussels, shrimp in shell, crab claws
2 tablespoons olive oil
2 leeks, sliced
2 stalks celery, sliced
2 onions, chopped
2 garlic cloves, chopped
4 tomatoes, chopped
1-1/4 cups dry white wine
8 oz. fish bones and heads
Bouquet garni
1 teaspoon saffron strands
Salt and freshly ground pepper
1/2 loaf of French bread
1 cup grated Gruyère cheese
Flat-leaf parsley sprigs, to garnish
ROUILLE:
2/3 cup mayonnaise
2 hard-cooked egg yolks
2 teaspoons harissa or chile paste

Trim mussels (see page 99). Heat olive oil in a
large saucepan. Add leeks, celery, onions and
garlic and cook, stirring occasionally, 10
minutes or until soft. Add tomatoes, wine, 4-
1/2 cups water, fish bones and heads,
shellfish, bouquet garni and saffron. Bring to
a boil, reduce heat, cover and simmer 30
minutes.

Preheat oven to 350F (180C). Slice French
bread and put on a baking sheet. Bake in
oven 15 to 20 minutes or until dried but not
browned. Let cool.

To make rouille, put mayonnaise into a bowl. Using a fork, mash egg yolks into mayonnaise. Stir in harissa or chile paste, adding more, if necessary, to give a fiery taste. Cover and refrigerate until required.

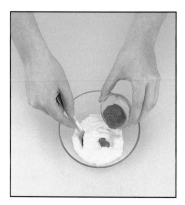

Strain shellfish mixture through a colander into a clean saucepan, pressing out as much liquid as possible. Discard contents of colander. Add fish to strained cooking liquid, bring to a boil, reduce heat and simmer 5 minutes or until fish is cooked through. Strain into a clean saucepan, reserving fish.

Put fish in a blender or food processor with 1-1/4 cups of the cooking liquid and process until well blended but still retaining some texture. Stir back into saucepan. Season with salt and pepper and reheat gently. Spread toasted French bread slices with rouille and float on top of soup. Sprinkle with grated cheese, garnish with flat-leaf parsley and serve.

Makes 8 servings.

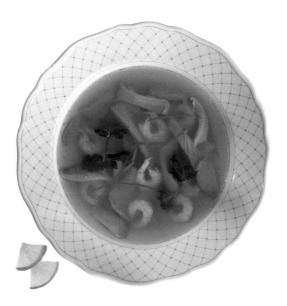

— HOT & SOUR SHRIMP SOUP —

8 oz. cooked large shrimp in shells
2 stalks lemon grass
6-1/4 cups vegetable stock
2 slices ginger root, peeled
4 kaffir lime leaves (optional)
1/4 cup Thai fish sauce
1/4 cup fresh lime juice
2 garlic cloves, very finely chopped
2 shallots, very finely chopped
1 fresh red chile, seeded and cut into thin strips
4 oz. oyster mushrooms, sliced
Cilantro sprigs, to garnish

Peel shrimp. Reserve shrimp and put shells into a large saucepan.

Lightly crush lemon grass and add to pan with stock, ginger root and lime leaves, if using. Bring to a boil, reduce heat and simmer 20 minutes. Strain into a clean saucepan, discarding shrimp shells and herbs.

Add fish sauce, lime juice, garlic, shallots, chile and mushrooms to pan. Bring to a boil, reduce heat and simmer 5 minutes. Add peeled shrimp and cook 1 minute, to heat through. Garnish with cilantro and serve.

Makes 6 servings.

SUMMER SALAD

3/4 cucumber
12 oz. strawberries (about 2-1/3 cups)
1 teaspoon pink peppercorns
Mint leaves, to garnish
DRESSING:
2 tablespoons balsamic vinegar
1/4 cup olive oil
Salt

To make dressing, mix together vinegar, olive oil and salt in a large bowl. Slice cucumber very thinly, using a mandoline or slicing disc on a food processor.

Put cucumber slices into bowl with dressing and mix gently to coat. Slice strawberries. Arrange a circle of overlapping slices of cucumber on serving plates.

Arrange strawberry slices in a circle inside cucumber, then arrange remaining cucumber slices inside strawberries. Place remaining strawberries in center. Lightly crush peppercorns and sprinkle over salads. Using scissors, snip mint leaves over salads and serve at once.

Makes 6 servings.

GREEN BEAN SALAD

3/4 cup dried flageolet beans, soaked overnight and
  drained
1 onion, quartered
1 carrot, quartered
Bouquet garni
6 oz. small green beans, halved (about 1-1/3 cups)
6 oz. shelled broad beans or lima beans (about 1 cup)
4 green onions, chopped
Chopped crispy bacon, to garnish
DRESSING:
1 tablespoon lemon juice
1/3 cup olive oil
1 teaspoon Dijon mustard
Salt and freshly ground pepper
1 tablespoon chopped fresh parsley
1 tablespoon chopped fresh tarragon

Put flageolet beans into a saucepan with
onion, carrot and bouquet garni. Cover with
cold water and bring to a boil. Boil rapidly 10
minutes, cover and simmer 1-1/2 hours, or
until beans are tender. To make dressing, put
all ingredients in a jar with a tight-fitting lid
and shake to mix thoroughly. Set aside.

Remove onion, carrot and bouquet garni
from beans and drain beans. Put beans into a
bowl, add dressing and mix gently. Let cool.
Cook green beans and broad beans in boiling
water 5 minutes or until tender. Drain
thoroughly and let cool. Add to flageolet
beans with green onions. Mix well to coat
with dressing. Garnish with crispy bacon and
serve.

Makes 6 servings.

SPINACH SALAD

12 cherry tomatoes
Salt and freshly ground pepper
1/4 cup olive oil
12 quail eggs
6 oz. young spinach leaves, rinsed and dried
4 slices bacon
1 tablespoon balsamic vinegar

Preheat oven to 400F (205C). Cut tomatoes in half and arrange in a roasting pan. Season with salt and pepper and drizzle 2 tablespoons of the olive oil over tomatoes. Bake 15 to 20 minutes, basting occasionally, until tender. Set aside.

Bring a saucepan of water to a boil. Gently add quail eggs to water and cook 3 minutes. Drain eggs, place in a bowl of cold water and let cool. Arrange spinach leaves on serving plates.

Peel eggs and cut in half. Arrange on spinach leaves. Remove tomatoes from roasting pan with a slotted spoon and arrange on spinach leaves. Cut bacon into strips. Heat remaining oil in a skillet, add bacon strips and cook 5 minutes or until golden. Remove bacon with a slotted spoon and scatter over salads. Add balsamic vinegar to tomato juices in roasting pan and mix together. Pour over salads and serve.

Makes 6 servings.

—BROILED BELL PEPPER SALAD—

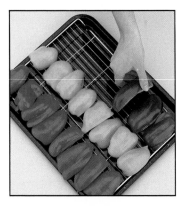

2 each red, green and yellow bell peppers
3 tablespoons olive oil
1 (2-oz.) can anchovies in olive oil
Freshly ground pepper
2 teaspoons capers
12 pitted ripe olives, halved
Flat-leaf parsley sprigs, to garnish

Preheat broiler. Cut bell peppers into quarters and remove cores and seeds. Place bell peppers on broiler rack, skin side up. Broil 5 to 10 minutes or until skins are charred and blistered.

Put bell peppers in a plastic bag, seal and leave until cool enough to handle. Peel bell peppers and cut flesh into thin strips.

Put olive oil into a large bowl. Drain oil from anchovies into olive oil. Season with black pepper. Put bell peppers into bowl with oil. Cut anchovies in half lengthwise. Add anchovies and capers to bell peppers and mix well. Let cool. Scatter with olives, garnish with flat-leaf parsley and serve.

Makes 6 servings.

Note: Anchovies can be quite salty, so extra salt is not needed in this salad.

-ANCHOVY & PARMESAN SALAD-

2 tablespoons olive oil
1 (2-oz.) can anchovies in olive oil
1 garlic clove
Pinch of cayenne pepper
4 slices white bread
9 oz. mixed salad greens
2 oz. Parmesan cheese
DRESSING:
1 tablespoon balsamic vinegar
1 teaspoon Dijon mustard
1/4 cup olive oil
Freshly ground pepper

Preheat oven to 375F (190C). Brush a baking sheet with 1 tablespoon of the olive oil.

Drain anchovies, reserving oil. Using a pestle and mortar, or in a blender or food processor, pound together anchovies, garlic, cayenne and remaining olive oil. Remove crusts from bread. Spread one side of each slice of bread with anchovy paste. Cut bread into 1/2-inch cubes and arrange, paste side up, on baking sheet. Bake 8 to 10 minutes or until crisp. Let cool.

To make dressing, in a large bowl, mix together vinegar, mustard, olive oil, reserved oil from anchovies and pepper. Add salad leaves and toss to coat thoroughly. Arrange salad greens on serving plates. Scatter anchovy croûtons over salads. Using a vegetable peeler, shave curls of Parmesan cheese over salads and serve.

Makes 6 servings.

—CRAB & AVOCADO SALAD—

12 oz. crabmeat
1 tablespoon fresh lime juice
Grated zest of 1 lime
1 tablespoon chopped fresh cilantro
Salt and freshly ground pepper
2 ripe avocados
9 oz. mixed salad greens
Lime slices and cilantro leaves, to garnish
LIME DRESSING:
1 tablespoon fresh lime juice
1/3 cup olive oil
1 tablespoon chopped fresh cilantro
1/2 teaspoon sugar

To make lime dressing, in a large bowl, mix together lime juice, olive oil, cilantro, sugar, salt and pepper. In another bowl, mix together crabmeat, lime juice, lime zest, cilantro, salt and pepper. Halve avocados lengthwise, remove pits and peel. Cut avocado flesh into 1/2-inch cubes.

Put salad leaves into bowl with dressing and toss to coat thoroughly. Arrange salad leaves on serving plates. Put a spoonful of crab mixture in center of each plate. Arrange diced avocado around crab mixture. Garnish with slices of lime and cilantro leaves and serve.

Makes 6 servings.

— ROAST VEGETABLE SALAD —

1 large eggplant
4 zucchini
1 yellow and 2 red bell peppers
2 small fennel bulbs
12 cherry tomatoes
2 garlic cloves, crushed
2 teaspoons pesto
1/2 cup olive oil
1 teaspoon coarse sea salt
1 tablespoon fresh lemon juice
Freshly ground pepper
Basil sprigs, to garnish

Preheat oven to 400F (205C). Slice eggplant and cut into chunks. Cut zucchini into chunks.

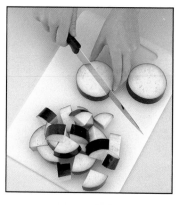

Quarter bell peppers and remove cores and seeds. Trim fennel and cut lengthwise into quarters. Cut a cross in the bottom of each tomato. In a bowl, mix together garlic, pesto and olive oil. Arrange vegetables in a large, heavy roasting pan. Add pesto mixture and toss vegetables to coat. Sprinkle with sea salt.

Roast 45 minutes, or until vegetables are browned and tender. Drizzle with lemon juice and season with black pepper. Leave in pan until tepid or cold. Garnish with basil sprigs and serve.

Makes 6 servings.

TROPICAL SALAD

3 pink grapefruit
1 large papaya
3 avocados
3 tablespoons olive oil
2 teaspoons pink peppercorns, lightly crushed
Salt

Cut zest from pink grapefruit, removing white pith at the same time. Hold grapefruit over a bowl to catch juice and cut between membranes to remove segments.

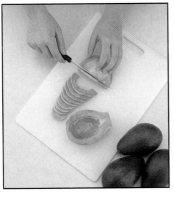

Peel papaya, cut in half and scoop out seeds with a teaspoon. Cut flesh into thin slices. Halve avocados lengthwise, remove pits and peel. Cut flesh into thin slices.

Arrange grapefruit segments, papaya slices and avocado slices on serving plates. Mix together 2 teaspoons reserved grapefruit juice, olive oil, crushed peppercorns and salt. Drizzle over fruit and serve at once.

Makes 6 servings.

———— CHICKEN & PEAR SALAD ————

3 oz. arugula
3 oz. watercress
3 ripe pears
1/4 cup butter
2 tablespoons sunflower oil
12 oz. cooked smoked chicken breast, cubed
1 cup walnut pieces
2 oz. Parmesan cheese
WALNUT DRESSING:
2 teaspoons white wine vinegar
2 tablespoons each walnut oil and sunflower oil
Salt and freshly ground pepper

To make dressing, in a large bowl, whisk together vinegar, walnut oil, sunflower oil, salt and pepper.

Put arugula and watercress into bowl with dressing and toss to coat thoroughly. Arrange on serving plates. Peel and quarter pears and remove cores. Cut each pear quarter lengthwise in half. Heat half the butter and half the sunflower oil in a skillet. Add pears and cook, turning occasionally, until just beginning to brown around edges.

Meanwhile, heat remaining butter and oil in another skillet. Add chicken and cook, stirring, until heated through. Add walnuts and heat through. Arrange pears, chicken and walnuts on top of arugula and watercress. Using a vegetable peeler, shave curls of Parmesan cheese over salads and serve.

Makes 6 servings.

INSALATA TRICOLORE

12 oz. cherry tomatoes
2 avocados
8 oz. mozzarella cheese
6 cup-shaped lettuce leaves
Fresh chives, to garnish
DRESSING:
1 tablespoon lemon juice
1/3 cup olive oil
1 teaspoon Dijon mustard
Salt and freshly ground pepper

To make dressing, in a large bowl, whisk together lemon juice, olive oil, mustard, salt and pepper. Cut cherry tomatoes in half and place in bowl with dressing.

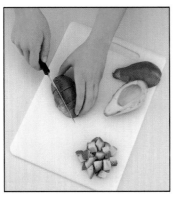

Halve avocados lengthwise, remove pits and peel. Cut avocado flesh and mozzarella cheese into 3/4-inch cubes. Add to tomatoes. Mix gently to coat with dressing.

Place lettuce 'cups' on serving plates and fill with tomato, avocado and mozzarella mixture. Garnish with chives and serve.

Makes 6 servings.

DUCK & LENTIL SALAD

1-1/4 cups Puy lentils
1 onion
1 garlic clove
1 bay leaf
6 green onions, thinly sliced
2 tablespoons olive oil
2 duck breasts
Chopped fresh parsley, to garnish
MUSTARD DRESSING:
2 garlic cloves, crushed
1 tablespoon whole-grain mustard
1 tablespoon balsamic vinegar
1/3 cup olive oil
Salt and freshly ground pepper

To make dressing, put garlic, mustard, vinegar, olive oil, salt and pepper in a jar with a tight-fitting lid and shake to mix thoroughly. Rinse lentils and put into a saucepan with onion, garlic and bay leaf. Cover with cold water and bring to a boil. Reduce heat, cover and simmer 15 minutes, or until tender. Remove and discard onion, garlic and bay leaf and drain lentils.

Put lentils into a bowl, add green onions and mustard dressing. Mix gently. Heat oil in a skillet, add duck and fry 5 minutes on each side or until still slightly pink in the center and skin is crisp. Thinly slice. Transfer lentils to serving plates and arrange duck on top. Garnish with chopped parsley and serve.

Makes 6 servings.

Note: Puy lentils are high-quality, gray-green lentils. Use green or brown lentils if Puy lentils are not available.

SESAME NOODLE SALAD

7 oz. fine rice noodles
1 carrot
4 green onions, sliced
1 tablespoon toasted sesame seeds
Cilantro sprigs, to garnish
SESAME DRESSING:
5 teaspoons sesame paste
5 teaspoons sesame oil
5 teaspoons soy sauce
2 tablespoons rice vinegar
1 teaspoon sugar
1 teaspoon grated ginger root
Salt and freshly ground pepper

Soak noodles as directed on package, until soft. Drain and set aside.

Cut carrot into 1-inch long matchsticks. Blanch in boiling water 1 minute. Drain, rinse in cold water, drain again and set aside.

To make sesame dressing, in a large bowl, mix together sesame paste, sesame oil, soy sauce, rice vinegar, sugar, ginger root, salt and pepper. Add noodles and toss to coat thoroughly. Stir in carrot and green onions. Sprinkle with sesame seeds, garnish with cilantro sprigs and serve at once.

Makes 6 servings.

Variation: Add cooked, peeled large shrimp or diced ham before serving.

BULGHUR SALAD

1 cup bulghur wheat
1 red bell pepper
1 bunch of green onions
2 large tomatoes
3 oz. fresh parsley (about 1 cup)
1 oz. fresh mint (about 1/3 cup)
Juice of 1 lemon
1/4 cup olive oil
Salt and freshly ground pepper
6 large, cup-shaped radicchio leaves
Mint leaves and flat-leaf parsley sprigs, to garnish

Put bulghur into a bowl, cover with warm water and leave to soak 30 minutes.

Turn bulghur into a colander and let drain. Dice bell pepper and blanch in boiling water 1 minute. Drain, rinse in cold water and drain again. Slice green onions. Put tomatoes in a bowl, cover with boiling water and leave 1 minute. Transfer to a bowl of cold water and leave 1 minute. Peel and coarsely chop tomatoes. Chop parsley and mint.

Put bulghur, bell pepper, green onions, tomatoes, parsley and mint into a large bowl. Add lemon juice, olive oil, salt and pepper and mix thoroughly. Let stand 1 hour. Pile into radicchio leaves, garnish with mint leaves and flat-leaf parsley sprigs and serve.

Makes 6 servings.

Variation: The salad can also be used to fill hollowed-out tomatoes.

——GREEN & GOLD ROULADE——

1 lb. carrots, sliced
1/2 cup cream cheese, softened
Salt and freshly ground pepper
1 lb. frozen chopped spinach
4 eggs, separated
Large pinch of grated nutmeg
Flat-leaf parsley sprigs and carrot ribbons, to garnish
HERB SAUCE:
3/4 cup crème fraîche
1 tablespoon chopped fresh parsley
3 tablespoons chopped fresh chives
Chopped fresh chives, to garnish

Cook carrots in a saucepan of boiling salted water 15 minutes or until tender. Drain.

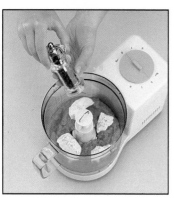

Purée carrots in a blender or food processor. Add cream cheese, salt and pepper and process until well blended. Set aside.

Preheat oven to 400F (205C). Lightly oil a 13- x 9-inch jelly roll pan and line with parchment paper. Lightly oil parchment paper. Cook spinach according to package directions. Drain well, pressing out as much water as possible. Place in a bowl and let cool slightly. Stir in egg yolks, nutmeg, salt and pepper.

In a large bowl, whisk egg whites until soft peaks form, then fold into spinach mixture. Gently spread into prepared pan and bake 15 to 20 minutes or until firm.

Meanwhile, make herb sauce. Mix together crème fraîche, parsley and chives, cover and refrigerate until required. Gently reheat carrot mixture without boiling. Turn spinach roll onto a sheet of parchment paper, peel off lining paper and spread spinach roll with carrot mixture.

Roll up by gently lifting parchment paper. Garnish herb sauce with chopped chives. Garnish roulade with flat-leaf parsley and carrot ribbons, slice and serve on warmed plates with herb sauce.

Makes 6 servings.

—CARROT & CELERIAC SALADS—

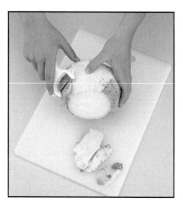

1 large celeriac
2/3 cup mayonnaise
4 teaspoons Dijon mustard
1/3 cup olive oil
1 tablespoon tarragon vinegar
1 garlic clove, crushed
Salt and freshly ground pepper
1 lb. carrots
2 tablespoons chopped fresh parsley
Parsley sprigs, to garnish
ANCHOVY TOAST:
6 anchovies
1/4 cup butter, softened
4 slices white bread, crusts removed

Trim and peel celeriac. Coarsely grate.

Immediately mix celeriac with mayonnaise and mustard. In a large bowl, whisk together olive oil, vinegar, garlic, salt and pepper. Finely grate carrot and mix into dressing. Stir in parsley. Arrange celeriac and carrot mixtures on serving plates.

Preheat broiler. To make anchovy toast, mash together anchovies and butter. Toast bread on one side. Spread untoasted side with anchovy butter and broil until crisp. Cut toast into fingers. Garnish salads with parsley and serve with anchovy toast.

Makes 6 servings.

—AVOCADO & RED CURRANTS—

3 ripe avocados
Red currants, to garnish
DRESSING:
6 oz. red currants
2 tablespoons balsamic vinegar
1/2 cup light olive oil or sunflower oil
Salt and freshly ground pepper
1/2 to 1 teaspoon sugar

To make dressing, purée red currants in a blender or food processor. Press through a nylon strainer to remove seeds.

Return red currant purée to blender with vinegar. With motor running, gradually pour in oil. Season with salt and pepper and add sugar to taste.

Halve avocados lengthwise. Remove pits and peel. Thinly slice flesh lengthwise. Fan out slices on serving plates. Stir dressing and pour around avocados. Garnish with red currants and serve immediately.

Makes 6 servings.

Note: Be sure to use a nylon strainer as a metal one may taint the flavor of the red currants.

RATATOUILLE TERRINE

12 large spinach or Swiss chard leaves
Salt and freshly ground pepper
3 yellow bell peppers, quartered
3 red bell peppers, quartered
1 garlic clove, crushed
1/2 cup olive oil
2 eggplant
4 zucchini
Red and yellow bell pepper strips and flat-leaf
    parsley sprigs, to garnish
2 tomatoes, peeled, seeded and diced, to serve
TOMATO VINAIGRETTE:
1 large ripe tomato
4 teaspoons balsamic vinegar
1/2 cup olive oil

Remove spinach stems and rinse leaves thoroughly. Blanch spinach in boiling water 1 minute. Drain, rinse in cold water and drain again. Spread spinach leaves on a clean dish towel, place another dish towel on top and pat dry. Line a 4-1/2-cup terrine or loaf pan with plastic wrap. Line terrine with blanched spinach leaves, leaving ends overhanging sides of terrine. Season lightly with salt and pepper.

Preheat broiler. Broil and peel bell peppers (see page 30). Mix together garlic and olive oil. Cut zucchini and eggplant lengthwise into 1/2-inch slices. Brush with garlic oil and broil on both sides until soft and beginning to brown.

Put a layer of yellow bell peppers in bottom of lined terrine, then add a layer of red bell peppers, followed by layers of eggplant, zucchini, red bell pepper, eggplant, zucchini, finishing with a layer of yellow bell pepper. Lightly season each layer with salt and pepper.

Fold overhanging spinach over top of terrine. Cover with plastic wrap. Press down with a weight and refrigerate 8 hours.

To make tomato vinaigrette, put tomato, vinegar, olive oil, salt and pepper in a blender or food processor and process until smooth. Press through a strainer. Turn terrine onto a serving dish and remove plastic wrap. Garnish with bell pepper strips. Slice terrine with a very sharp knife, garnish with flat-leaf parsley and serve with tomato vinaigrette and diced tomato.

Makes 6 to 8 servings.

CAPONATA

2 eggplant
Salt and freshly ground pepper
1/2 cup olive oil
1 onion, finely chopped
1 garlic clove, chopped
4 stalks celery, sliced, leaves reserved for garnish
1 (14-oz.) can crushed tomatoes
2 teaspoons sugar
2 tablespoons balsamic vinegar
1 tablespoon pine nuts, lightly toasted
1 tablespoon capers
12 pitted ripe olives, halved

Cut eggplant into 1/4-inch thick slices.

Place eggplant in a colander, sprinkle generously with salt and leave 1 hour. Preheat oven to 300F (150C). Heat 2 tablespoons olive oil in a saucepan, add onion and garlic and cook, stirring occasionally, 5 minutes or until soft. Add celery and cook, stirring occasionally, another 5 minutes. Stir in tomatoes, sugar and vinegar and bring to a boil. Simmer, uncovered, 15 to 20 minutes or until thickened. Season with salt and pepper and stir in pine nuts, capers and olives.

Rinse eggplant thoroughly and pat dry with paper towels. Arrange in a shallow ovenproof dish. Spoon a little tomato mixture onto each eggplant slice. Drizzle remaining oil over and around eggplant. Cover with foil and cook in oven 45 to 60 minutes or until eggplant are tender. Let cool. Garnish with celery leaves and serve at room temperature.

Makes 6 servings.

ASPARAGUS TARTLETS

1 lb. asparagus, cooked
1 egg
1 egg yolk
2/3 cup half-and-half
Salt and freshly ground pepper
1/2 cup freshly grated Parmesan cheese
Basil sprigs, to garnish
PASTRY:
3 cups all-purpose flour
1/3 cup butter, diced
1/3 cup solid vegetable shortening, diced
2-1/2 tablespoons cold water

To make pastry, sift flour into a bowl. Rub in butter and shortening until mixture resembles fine bread crumbs.

Stir in cold water to bind to a smooth dough. Wrap in plastic wrap and refrigerate 30 minutes. Preheat oven to 400F (205C). Thinly roll out pastry on a lightly floured surface. Cut circles to fit six 4-inch loose-bottomed tartlet pans. Line pans with pastry, then press foil into pastry cases. Fill with dried beans and bake 15 minutes. Remove beans and foil and let cool slightly. Reduce oven temperature to 350F (180C).

Cut 3-inch lengths from tips of asparagus and reserve. Snap woody ends off asparagus stalks and peel off any tough skin. Purée asparagus stalks in a blender or food processor. Add egg, egg yolk and half-and-half and blend until smooth. Stir in salt and pepper and Parmesan cheese. Pour mixture into pastry cases and arrange asparagus tips on top. Bake 20 minutes or until set and golden. Garnish with basil and serve warm with salad greens.

Makes 6 servings.

—MUSHROOM BRIOCHES—

6 small brioches
1/3 cup olive oil
1 garlic clove, crushed
2 shallots, finely chopped
12 oz. mixed mushrooms, sliced
1 teaspoon Dijon mustard
2 tablespoons dry sherry
1 tablespoon chopped fresh tarragon
2/3 cup whipping cream
Salt and freshly ground pepper
Watercress, to garnish

Preheat oven to 400F (205C). Pull tops off brioches and scoop out insides of each brioche to make a hollow case.

Brush insides of brioches with 3 tablespoons of the olive oil. Arrange brioches on a baking sheet and bake 10 to 12 minutes or until crisp. Meanwhile, heat remaining oil in a saucepan, add garlic and shallots and cook, stirring occasionally, 3 minutes or until soft. Add mushrooms and cook over low heat, stirring occasionally, 5 minutes.

Stir in mustard, sherry, tarragon, cream, salt and pepper. Cook for a few minutes or until cream reduces and thickens slightly. Fill brioche cases with mushroom mixture, garnish with watercress and serve at once.

Makes 6 servings.

CRISPY WON TONS

1 red bell pepper
1 carrot
5 green onions
4 oz. each button mushrooms and bean sprouts
2-1/2 cups sunflower oil
1 teaspoon grated ginger root
1 teaspoon sugar
1 teaspoon each soy sauce and sesame oil
2 teaspoons sherry
24 won-ton skins
DIPPING SAUCE:
6 tablespoons fresh lime juice
2 teaspoons sugar
1 teaspoon Thai fish sauce
1 teaspoon finely chopped green onion
1 fresh green chile, cored, seeded and chopped

To make dipping sauce, mix together lime juice, sugar, fish sauce, green onion and chile. Stir until sugar has dissolved. Set aside. Cut bell pepper and carrot into thin matchsticks. Shred green onions, reserving a few shreds for garnish. Thinly slice mushrooms. Heat 2 tablespoons of the sunflower oil in a wok and stir-fry bell pepper, carrot, green onions, mushrooms, bean sprouts and ginger root 1 minute. Add sugar, soy sauce, sesame oil and sherry and cook, stirring, 2 minutes. Turn into a strainer and leave to drain and cool.

Put 1 teaspoon vegetable mixture in the middle of each won-ton skin. Gather up corners and twist together to seal. In a wok or deep-fat fryer, heat oil to 180C (350F) or until a cube of bread browns in 60 seconds. Fry won tons, a few at a time, 1 or 2 minutes, until crisp and golden. Remove with a slotted spoon and drain on paper towels. Keep warm while frying remaining won tons. Garnish with reserved green onion shreds and serve with dipping sauce.

Makes 6 servings.

—SPINACH & GARLIC TERRINE—

1 lb. frozen chopped spinach, thawed
3 green onions, sliced
2 garlic cloves, crushed
3/4 cup shredded Cheddar cheese
8 oz. crème fraîche
3 eggs, beaten
Salt and freshly ground pepper
Watercress sprigs, to garnish
TOMATO SALAD:
2 teaspoons white wine vinegar
3 tablespoons olive oil
18 cherry tomatoes, halved

Preheat oven to 350F (180C). Lightly oil a 4-1/2-cup terrine or loaf pan.

Line bottom and narrow ends of loaf pan with a strip of parchment paper. Press as much water as possible out of spinach and place in a blender or food processor. Add green onions, garlic, Cheddar cheese, crème fraîche, eggs, salt and pepper. Process until thoroughly blended. Pour mixture into prepared pan and cover with oiled foil.

Place terrine in a roasting pan and add boiling water to come half-way up sides of terrine. Cook in the oven 1 hour, or until a skewer inserted into the center comes out clean. Let cool in roasting pan. Pour any excess liquid from terrine, then refrigerate at least 2 hours. To make tomato salad, whisk together vinegar, oil, salt and pepper. Toss tomatoes in dressing. Turn out terrine and slice. Garnish with watercress and serve with tomato salad.

Makes 6 servings.

BAGNA CAUDA

2 carrots
1 red bell pepper
3 baby eggplant
Olive oil for brushing
1 fennel bulb
24 cherry tomatoes
Loaf of French bread, sliced
ANCHOVY & GARLIC DIP:
2 garlic cloves
2 (2-oz.) cans anchovies in olive oil, drained
1/2 cup butter
2/3 cup olive oil

Cut carrots and bell pepper into sticks. Preheat broiler.

Cut baby eggplant in half, brush with olive oil and broil 5 to 7 minutes or until soft. Cut fennel lengthwise into quarters, reserving top for garnish. Arrange vegetables on serving plates with French bread slices.

To make dip, using a pestle and mortar, pound garlic and anchovies to a paste. Heat butter and oil in a saucepan. Add anchovy paste and cook 10 minutes, stirring occasionally. Transfer to a bagna cauda pot or small fondue pot and keep warm. Garnish vegetables with fennel sprigs and serve with warm anchovy dip.

Makes 6 servings.

Variation: Any selection of breads or vegetables can be served with a bagna cauda.

——— VEGETABLE TEMPURA ———

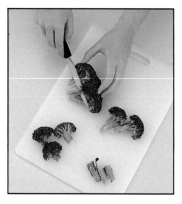

2 lbs. mixed vegetables, including broccoli, carrots, red bell peppers, zucchini, baby eggplant, button mushrooms
2 tablespoons all-purpose flour
Sunflower oil for deep-frying
DIPPING SAUCE:
1-inch piece ginger root, peeled and grated
1/3 cup dry sherry
1/4 cup soy sauce
3/4 cup boiling water
BATTER:
2 large eggs
About 1 cup iced water
1 cup all-purpose flour

Cut broccoli into small flowerets.

Cut carrots and bell peppers into strips. Slice zucchini and eggplant. To make dipping sauce, mix together ginger root, sherry, soy sauce and boiling water. Mix well, then set aside. To make batter, put eggs into a bowl with scant cup iced water and beat until frothy.

Add flour and beat until just blended. Don't worry if a few lumps are left. Stand bowl in a bowl of ice. Toss vegetables in flour. Heat oil in a wok or deep-fat fryer to 190C (375F) or until a cube of bread browns in 40 seconds. Using a fork, dip floured vegetables in batter and add to the hot oil, in batches. Deep-fry 3 to 5 minutes or until crisp and golden. Remove with a slotted spoon, drain on paper towels and keep warm while frying remaining batches. Serve with dipping sauce.

Makes 6 servings.

PARMESAN ASPARAGUS

1/4 cup olive oil
1-1/2 teaspoons coarse sea salt
1-1/2 lbs. asparagus
Freshly ground pepper
2 hard-cooked eggs, chopped
2 oz. Parmesan cheese
Lemon wedges

Preheat oven to 350F (180C). Grease an ovenproof dish with a little of the olive oil. Sprinkle with half the salt.

Snap woody ends off asparagus stalks and peel tough skin from bottom 2 inches of stalks, if necessary. Arrange asparagus in prepared dish and drizzle with remaining oil. Turn asparagus in oil and sprinkle with remaining salt. Roast 10 to 15 minutes or until tender. Transfer to warmed serving plates.

Season with pepper and sprinkle with chopped eggs. Using a vegetable peeler, shave curls of Parmesan over asparagus. Serve immediately with lemon wedges.

Makes 6 servings.

CHEESY QUESADILLAS

1-1/2 lbs. tomatoes
1/4 cup sunflower oil
1 large onion, finely sliced
1 fresh green chile, cored, seeded and chopped
2 tablespoons tomato paste
1 vegetable stock cube
1 (8-oz.) can whole-kernel corn, drained
1 tablespoon chopped fresh cilantro
6 flour tortillas
1 cup shredded Cheddar cheese
Flat-leaf parsley sprigs, to garnish
Shredded lettuce

Put tomatoes into a bowl, cover with boiling water and leave 1 minute. Drain and plunge into a bowl of cold water.

Leave 1 minute, then drain. Peel tomatoes, remove seeds and chop flesh. Heat half the oil in a skillet. Add onion and cook, stirring occasionally, 5 minutes or until soft. Add tomatoes, chile, tomato paste and stock cube and cook over low heat 5 minutes or until chile is soft but tomato has not completely broken down. Stir in corn and cilantro and heat gently to warm through. Keep warm.

Sprinkle each tortilla with cheese, leaving a 1/2-inch border. Spoon some tomato mixture over cheese. Fold tortilla in half to enclose filling. Heat remaining oil in a skillet. Place two or three tortillas in skillet and cook 1 or 2 minutes on each side, until golden and crisp. Keep warm while cooking remaining tortillas. Garnish with parsley sprigs and serve on a bed of shredded lettuce.

Makes 6 servings.

─── VEGETABLE CROSTINI ───

1 zucchini
1 small eggplant
1 small red bell pepper
1 small fennel bulb
2 garlic cloves, crushed
1 teaspoon chopped fresh thyme
1/4 cup olive oil
Salt and freshly ground pepper
12 slices ciabatta, toasted
10 oz. mozzarella cheese
Thyme sprigs, to garnish

Cut zucchini, eggplant and bell pepper into 1/2-inch pieces. Coarsely chop fennel.

Preheat broiler. In a bowl, mix together zucchini, eggplant, bell pepper, fennel, garlic, thyme, oil, salt and pepper. Spread vegetables in a broiler pan and broil 12 to 15 minutes, turning frequently, until tender and beginning to brown at edges.

Slice cheese and arrange on toasted ciabatta. Pile broiled vegetables on top of cheese. Broil 2 or 3 minutes or until cheese is beginning to bubble. Garnish with thyme sprigs and serve at once.

Makes 6 servings.

——STUFFED MUSHROOMS——

6 large flat mushrooms
4 thick slices olive ciabatta
6 sun-dried tomatoes in oil
4 oz. mozzarella cheese
1 tablespoon chopped fresh tarragon
1/4 cup olive oil
Salt and freshly ground pepper
Tarragon sprigs, to garnish

Preheat oven to 400F (205C). Lightly oil a baking sheet. Peel mushrooms, remove stalks and reserve.

In a food processor, process bread until it forms fine crumbs. Coarsely chop tomatoes. Cut cheese into small dice. Chop mushroom stalks. In a bowl, mix together bread crumbs, chopped tomatoes, cheese, mushroom stalks, tarragon, olive oil, salt and pepper.

Divide mixture among mushroom caps, pressing down firmly. Put mushrooms on baking sheet and bake 20 minutes or until mushrooms are cooked and stuffing is crisp on top. Garnish with tarragon and serve.

Makes 6 servings.

—— ZUCCHINI TIMBALES ——

1-1/2 lbs. zucchini
3 eggs, beaten
1 tablespoon chopped fresh basil
1/2 cup ricotta cheese
Salt and freshly ground pepper
TOMATO SALSA:
12 oz. tomatoes, peeled and diced (page 54)
1 red onion, finely chopped
1 tablespoon chopped fresh basil
1 tablespoon olive oil
1 teaspoon lime juice

To make tomato salsa, mix together tomatoes, onion, basil, olive oil, lime juice, salt and pepper. Refrigerate until required.

Oil 6 (1/2-cup) ramekins. Trim ends from zucchini. Using a vegetable peeler, cut very thin ribbons from two of the zucchini. Cut remaining zucchini into slices. Steam ribbons over boiling water 2 minutes or until soft. Spread on paper towels and pat dry. Steam sliced zucchini 3 to 5 minutes or until soft. Preheat oven to 400F (205C).

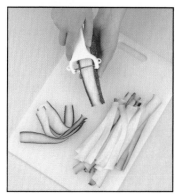

Press out as much moisture as possible from zucchini slices and place in a blender or food processor with eggs, basil, ricotta, salt and pepper. Process to a coarse purée. Line ramekins with zucchini strips. Fill with purée, fold ends of zucchini strips over filling and cover with foil. Place ramekins in a roasting pan and pour in 1/2-inch boiling water. Bake 10 to 15 minutes or until set. Leave 5 minutes, turn out and serve with tomato salsa.

Makes 6 servings.

QUICK TOMATO TARTS

10 oz. puff pastry, thawed if frozen
2 tablespoons pesto
10 plum tomatoes, thinly sliced crosswise
2 tablespoons olive oil
Salt and freshly ground pepper
4 oz. feta cheese
Basil sprigs, to garnish

Preheat oven to 425F (220C). Oil three baking sheets. Thinly roll out pastry on a lightly floured surface. Cut out 6 (6-inch) circles.

Place circles on hot baking sheets. Spread 1 teaspoon pesto over each pastry circle, leaving a 3/4-inch margin all round.

Arrange tomatoes slices, overlapping, on top of pesto. Drizzle olive oil over tomatoes, season with salt and pepper and crumble feta cheese over tarts. Bake 15 minutes or until golden and well risen. Garnish with basil sprigs and serve at once.

Makes 6 servings.

EGGPLANT ROLLS

2 eggplant, each weighing 9 oz.
1/4 cup olive oil
10 oz. ricotta cheese, drained
3/4 cup grated Parmesan cheese
1 oz. pine nuts, toasted
1 tablespoon chopped fresh basil
Salt and freshly ground pepper
Basil sprigs, to garnish
TOMATO SAUCE:
1 tablespoon olive oil
1 onion, finely chopped
1 garlic clove, crushed
1 (14-oz.) can crushed tomatoes
2/3 cup dry white wine

To make tomato sauce, heat olive oil in a saucepan, add onion and garlic and cook over low heat, stirring occasionally, 5 minutes or until soft. Add tomatoes, wine, salt and pepper. Bring to a boil, reduce heat and simmer 30 minutes, stirring occasionally. Add water if mixture becomes too dry. Meanwhile, preheat broiler. Cut eggplant lengthwise into 18 thin slices. Brush slices with oil, then broil, turning once, until soft.

Preheat oven to 375F (190C). Mix together cheeses, pine nuts, basil, salt and pepper. Put a spoonful of filling on one end of each eggplant slice and roll up. Place rolls, seam side down, in an ovenproof dish. Bake 10 to 15 minutes or until heated through. Reheat sauce. Divide sauce among warmed serving plates, arrange rolls on top, garnish with basil sprigs and serve.

Makes 6 servings.

— ARTICHOKES WITH AÏOLI —

6 artichokes
1 teaspoon fresh lemon juice
1 slice lemon
1 teaspoon sunflower oil
AÏOLI:
2/3 cup mayonnaise
2 garlic cloves, crushed
1 teaspoon Dijon mustard

Cut off artichoke stalks and any tough leaves. Trim base so that artichokes will stand upright. Trim about 1/2 inch off leafy top with a sharp knife.

Add lemon juice to a large bowl of cold water and soak artichokes 20 to 30 minutes. Put artichokes into a pan of boiling salted water. Add lemon slice and oil and cook 30 to 40 minutes or until a bottom leaf can be pulled off easily. Drain artichokes, turn upside down on a rack and let cool.

To make aïoli, mix together mayonnaise, garlic and mustard. Pull out center leaves of artichokes, scrape out hairy chokes with a teaspoon and discard. Place artichokes on serving plates and serve with aïoli.

Makes 6 servings.

Variation: Artichokes may also be served with a vinaigrette dressing or a herb mayonnaise. Alternatively, serve hot, with melted butter or hollandaise sauce.

ASPARAGUS RISOTTO

5 cups vegetable stock
1 lb. thin asparagus
1/3 cup butter
1 onion, finely chopped
1-1/2 cups Arborio rice
Pinch of saffron strands
Juice of 1 lemon
Salt and freshly ground pepper
Flat-leaf parsley and strips of lemon zest, to garnish

In a large saucepan, heat stock until boiling. Keep at simmering point over low heat. Cut tips off asparagus and set aside.

Snap woody ends off asparagus stalks and peel off any tough skin. Cut stalks into 2-inch lengths. In a large heavy saucepan, heat 2 tablespoons of the butter. Add onion and cook, stirring occasionally, 5 minutes or until soft. Add rice and asparagus stalks and cook, stirring, 2 or 3 minutes. Add a ladleful of hot stock and cook over low heat, stirring frequently, until stock is absorbed. Continue to stir in stock in this way, a ladleful at a time.

When rice begins to look creamy, add saffron, lemon juice, salt and pepper. Continue adding stock and stirring until risotto is thick and creamy and rice is tender but not sticky. Meanwhile, put asparagus tips in a steamer and steam 5 minutes, or until tender. Just before serving, add asparagus tips and remaining butter to risotto and stir gently to combine. Garnish with parsley and lemon zest and serve.

Makes 6 servings.

NORI SUSHI

1 cup short-grain rice
1-1/4 cups cold water
1 small carrot
1/4 cucumber
1 egg
1 teaspoon sunflower oil
3 nori sheets, 8 inches square
Green onion curls and radish flowers, to garnish
Wasabi paste and soy sauce, to serve
DRESSING:
2 tablespoons rice vinegar
1 tablespoon sugar
1 teaspoon salt

Rinse rice in several changes of cold water until water runs clear. Transfer to a colander and leave to drain 1 hour. Put rice into a saucepan with the cold water. Cover and bring to a boil. Reduce heat, cover and cook over very low heat 20 minutes. Remove from heat and let stand, still covered, 15 minutes. To make dressing, put rice vinegar, sugar and salt in a bowl and stir until sugar dissolves. Spread rice on a large baking sheet and pour dressing over rice. Mix gently with a dampened wooden spoon and let cool. Do not chill.

Cut carrot into thin matchsticks and blanch in boiling water 1 minute. Drain, rinse in cold water and drain again. Cut cucumber into matchsticks. In a bowl, beat egg with 2 teaspoons cold water. Heat oil in a small omelet pan. Pour egg into pan and cook over medium heat, lifting edge of omelet as egg sets, to allow liquid egg to flow onto pan. When omelet is just set, transfer to a plate and let cool. Roll up omelet and cut into 1/4-inch strips.

Toast nori sheets by passing them over a gas flame or broiling on the lowest setting very lightly on both sides. Place a sheet of nori on a bamboo sushi mat or clean dish towel. With a dampened hand, spread one-third of rice over nori sheet, leaving a 1/2-inch margin along side closest to you and opposite side.

Unroll omelet strips. Arrange one-third along center of rice. Arrange one-third of carrot and cucumber sticks next to omelet, in neat rows, keeping as close to the center as possible. Using bamboo mat or dish towel, firmly roll up sushi. Repeat with remaining ingredients to make three rolls.

With a sharp knife, cut each sushi roll into six slices and arrange, cut side up, on serving plates. Garnish with green onion curls and radish flowers and serve with wasabi paste and small bowls of soy sauce.

Makes 6 servings.

Note: Wasabi is a very hot type of horseradish, traditionally served with Japanese dishes such as sushi and sashimi.

RISOTTO TIMBALES

3-1/4 cups chicken stock
2 tablespoons butter
1 tablespoon olive oil
1 onion, finely chopped
1 garlic clove, crushed
1-1/4 cups Arborio rice
2/3 cup dry white wine
Salt and freshly ground pepper
2 eggs, beaten
2 oz. Gorgonzola cheese
1/2 cup fresh bread crumbs
RED BELL PEPPER SALAD:
1 red bell pepper, peeled (page 30)
2 tablespoons olive oil
1 teaspoon wine vinegar

Heat stock until boiling. Keep at simmering point. In a large heavy saucepan, heat butter and olive oil. Add onion and garlic and cook, stirring occasionally, 5 minutes or until soft. Add rice and cook, stirring, 2 or 3 minutes. Add a ladleful of hot stock and cook over low heat, stirring frequently, until stock is absorbed. Continue to stir in stock in this way, a ladleful at a time. Add wine and cook, stirring, until risotto is thick and creamy and rice is tender. Season with salt and pepper. Cool slightly and stir in eggs. Let cool.

Preheat oven to 350F (180C). Butter 6 (2/3 cup) baking cups and coat with bread crumbs. Half fill each cup with risotto. Cut cheese into 6 cubes and put in each cup. Cover with risotto, pressing down firmly. Bake 20 minutes or until crisp. Leave 5 minutes. Cut bell pepper into strips. Mix together olive oil and vinegar and toss with bell pepper. Turn out risottos and serve with bell pepper salad.

Makes 6 servings.

— POLENTA WITH MUSHROOMS —

1/4 cup butter
2 shallots, finely chopped
1 garlic clove, crushed
1 lb. mixed mushrooms, sliced
1/4 teaspoon freshly grated nutmeg
2 teaspoons lemon juice
Salt and freshly ground pepper
1/2 cup crème fraîche
Chopped fresh parsley, to garnish
POLENTA:
2-1/4 cups water
1 teaspoon salt
3/4 cup polenta
2 tablespoons butter
Freshly ground pepper

To make polenta, put water into a large heavy saucepan. Add salt and bring to a boil. Pour in polenta in a fine stream, stirring vigorously in one direction only with a long wooden spoon. Simmer, stirring frequently, about 15 minutes, or until polenta is very thick and coming away from sides of pan. Remove from heat and stir in butter and pepper. Turn out onto a flat plate and spread into a circle 1/2-inch thick. Let cool. Cover and refrigerate at least 1 hour. Cut into six wedges.

Heat butter in a skillet. Add shallots and garlic and cook 3 minutes or until soft. Add mushrooms and cook over low heat 2 or 3 minutes. Stir in nutmeg, lemon juice, salt and pepper and cook until liquid has evaporated. Stir in crème fraîche and cook a few minutes or until thickened. Meanwhile, preheat broiler. Broil polenta 3 or 4 minutes on each side until crisp. Arrange polenta and mushrooms on serving plates, garnish with parsley and serve.

Makes 6 servings.

—SMOKED SALMON RAVIOLI—

4 oz. smoked salmon, chopped
4 oz. (1/2 cup) cream cheese
2 teaspoons fresh lemon juice
Salt and freshly ground pepper
Flat-leaf parsley and lemon slices, to garnish
PASTA:
2 cups bread flour
1/2 teaspoon salt
2 eggs, beaten
GREEN PEPPERCORN SAUCE:
2 tablespoons butter
2 shallots, finely chopped
1/2 cup white wine
2/3 cup half-and-half
2 teaspoons green peppercorns, lightly crushed

To make pasta, sift flour and salt into a food processor. Add eggs and process to a crumbly consistency. Gather dough together to form a ball, wrap in plastic wrap and set aside 30 minutes.

On a floured surface, roll out dough into 2 (12- x 9-inch) thin sheets. Cut each sheet into 12 (3-inch) squares.

Put smoked salmon in a bowl with cream cheese and lemon juice and mix well. Season with salt and pepper. Place a small spoonful of salmon mixture on each square of dough.

Fold over dough and press edges together to form triangles. Arrange ravioli on a clean kitchen towel and leave a few minutes to dry, turning frequently. To make peppercorn sauce, heat butter in a saucepan. Add shallots and cook over very low heat 10 minutes or until soft. Add wine and boil until reduced by half.

Add half-and-half and peppercorns. Season with salt and boil until slightly thickened. Keep warm, stirring from time to time. Bring a large pan of salted water to a boil, add ravioli, a few at a time, and cook 5 to 10 minutes or until just tender. Drain. Arrange ravioli on warmed serving plates. Add sauce, garnish with parsley and lemon slices and serve.

Makes 6 servings.

ROAST TOMATO PASTA

2 lbs. ripe tomatoes
2 garlic cloves, finely chopped
2 teaspoons dried thyme
Salt and freshly ground pepper
1/4 cup olive oil
3 shallots, chopped
12 oz. garlic and herb tagliatelle
Basil leaves, to garnish

Preheat oven to 325F (165C). Cut tomatoes in half and place, cut side up, on a baking sheet. Sprinkle with garlic, thyme, salt and pepper. Drizzle with half the olive oil.

Roast tomatoes 40 minutes or until soft. Heat remaining olive oil in a saucepan. Add shallots and cook, stirring occasionally, 5 minutes or until soft. Scrape tomato flesh from skins, add to shallots in pan, discarding skins, and set aside.

Cook tagliatelle in a large pan of boiling salted water as directed on package, until just tender. Reheat tomato sauce. Drain pasta and put into a bowl. Add sauce and toss lightly. Garnish with basil leaves and serve.

Makes 6 servings.

— LINGUINE WITH ANCHOVIES —

1/3 cup olive oil
1 garlic clove, crushed
1 (2-oz.) can anchovies in olive oil, drained and
    coarsely chopped
Freshly ground pepper
12 oz. linguine
1 cup fresh whole-wheat bread crumbs
1 tablespoon chopped fresh parsley

Cook linguine in a large pan of boiling salted water as directed on package, until just tender. Meanwhile, heat half the olive oil in a small saucepan. Add garlic and cook over low heat, stirring occasionally, 2 or 3 minutes. Add anchovies and cook over low heat, stirring, until they melt into the oil. Season with pepper.

Heat remaining oil in a skillet, add bread crumbs and cook, stirring, until crisp. Drain pasta and arrange on warmed serving plates. Pour anchovies and oil on to pasta, sprinkle with bread crumbs and parsley and serve immediately.

Makes 6 servings.

—SPAGHETTI WITH MUSSELS—

12 oz. spaghetti
2 tablespoons olive oil, plus extra for tossing
3 shallots, finely chopped
1 garlic clove, crushed
1/2 cup dry white wine
2 lbs. mussels, trimmed (page 99)
2/3 cup fish stock
Large pinch of saffron strands
1/4 cup butter, diced
Salt and freshly ground pepper
2 tablespoons chopped fresh parsley

Cook spaghetti in a large pan of boiling salted water as directed on package, until just tender. Drain, toss in a little oil and set aside.

Heat olive oil in a large saucepan. Add shallots and garlic and cook over low heat, stirring occasionally, 5 minutes or until soft. Add wine and bring to a boil. Add mussels, cover tightly and cook over high heat 4 or 5 minutes, shaking pan occasionally, until mussels open. Remove with a slotted spoon, discarding any that have not opened. Reserve about 18 whole mussels, remove remaining mussels from their shells and keep warm.

Add fish stock and saffron to cooking juices in pan. Bring to a boil and boil rapidly until reduced by one-third. Whisk in butter, a little at a time. Add pasta and toss to coat. Season with salt and pepper and cook over low heat to warm through. Stir in shelled mussels and parsley. Transfer to warmed serving plates, garnish with whole mussels and serve.

Makes 6 servings.

Note: Do not overcook the pasta as it continues to cook in its own heat.

STUFFED PASTA SHELLS

8 oz. large conchiglie
1 lb. spinach
2 (2-oz.) cans anchovies in olive oil
2 tablespoons olive oil
1 garlic clove, finely chopped
1 fresh red chile, cored, seeded and finely chopped
2 tablespoons fresh lemon juice
3/4 cup fresh bread crumbs
1/4 cup grated Parmesan cheese
Strips of lemon zest, to garnish

Cook pasta in a large pan of boiling salted water as directed on package, until just tender.

Meanwhile, wash spinach and put into a large saucepan with only the water that clings to the leaves. Cook 2 or 3 minutes or until wilted. Drain thoroughly, coarsely chop and set aside. Put anchovies and their oil in a saucepan with olive oil, garlic and chile. Cook over low heat, stirring occasionally, 5 minutes, or until anchovies break down to a smooth consistency. Stir in lemon juice, half the bread crumbs and spinach. Preheat oven to 400F (205C).

Drain pasta, rinse in cold water and drain again. Divide spinach mixture among shells. Brush an ovenproof dish with oil and arrange stuffed shells in dish. Sprinkle with remaining bread crumbs and Parmesan cheese and bake 8 minutes. Garnish with lemon zest and serve immediately.

Makes 6 servings.

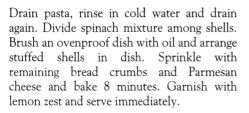

—PENNE WITH BELL PEPPERS—

3 red bell peppers
3 yellow bell peppers
1/4 cup olive oil
2 shallots, finely chopped
1 garlic clove, finely chopped
Salt and freshly ground pepper
12 oz. penne
2 teaspoons capers, chopped
1 teaspoon chopped fresh parsley
1 teaspoon chopped fresh tarragon

Preheat broiler. Cut bell peppers into quarters and remove cores and seeds. Place, skin side up, under a hot broiler and broil until skin is charred and blistered.

Put peppers into a plastic bag, seal and leave until cool enough to handle. Peel, then cut flesh into strips roughly the same size as the pasta. Heat oil in a saucepan, add shallots, garlic and bell peppers, cover and cook, stirring occasionally, 10 minutes. Remove lid and cook over high heat, stirring frequently, 5 minutes. Season with salt and pepper.

Meanwhile, cook pasta in a large pan of boiling salted water as directed on package, until just tender. Drain and return to saucepan. Stir in bell pepper mixture, capers, parsley and tarragon and serve.

Makes 6 servings.

—RIGATONI WITH ASPARAGUS—

1 lb. asparagus
1/2 cup crème fraîche
Salt and freshly ground pepper
2 tablespoons chopped fresh chives
12 oz. rigatoni
Chives, to garnish

Snap woody ends from asparagus stalks and peel off any tough skin. Cut off tips. Cut stalks into 1-inch pieces.

Add asparagus stalks to a saucepan of boiling salted water, put tips into a steamer and place above water. Simmer 10 minutes or until stalks are very tender. Remove tips and keep warm. Drain stalks, reserving cooking liquid. Put stalks into a blender or food processor with 2/3 cup cooking liquid and crème fraîche. Process until smooth.

Return purée to pan and reheat gently. Season with salt and pepper and stir in chives. Meanwhile, cook pasta in a large pan of boiling salted water as directed on package, until just tender. Drain and arrange on warmed serving plates. Add sauce, garnish with asparagus tips and chives and serve immediately.

Makes 6 servings.

—CHEESE & TOMATO FUSILLI—

12 oz. fusilli
1/4 cup olive oil
1 bunch green onions, chopped
1 garlic clove
Salt and freshly ground pepper
8 oz. cherry tomatoes, quartered
5 oz. mozzarella cheese, diced
1/2 cup grated Parmesan cheese
1 small bunch of basil
12 pitted ripe olives, halved

Cook pasta in a large pan of boiling salted water as directed on package, until just tender.

Meanwhile, heat olive oil in a small saucepan. Add green onions and cook, stirring occasionally, 2 or 3 minutes. Add garlic and cook 2 minutes. Drain pasta and return to saucepan. Add green onion mixture, salt and pepper.

Add tomatoes to pasta and stir over low heat, to warm through. Stir in cheeses. Coarsely tear basil leaves in halves or thirds, add to pasta with olives and serve immediately.

Makes 6 servings.

———— SPINACH TAGLIATELLE ————

10 oz. spinach
2 tablespoons olive oil
1 garlic clove, peeled
2/3 cup whipping cream
4 oz. mascarpone cheese
Salt and freshly ground pepper
12 oz. tagliatelle

Wash and dry spinach and chop very finely. Heat oil in a large saucepan. Add garlic and cook until browned. Remove with a slotted spoon and discard. Add spinach to pan and cook, stirring, 2 or 3 minutes or until wilted and tender.

Put cream, cheese, salt and pepper into a saucepan and bring to a boil. Simmer for a few minutes to thicken. Meanwhile, cook tagliatelle in a large pan of boiling salted water as directed on package, until just tender.

Drain pasta, reserving cooking water, and return to saucepan. Add enough of cooking liquid to cream sauce to give a smooth pouring consistency. Pour onto pasta. Add spinach and toss to coat. Serve immediately.

Makes 6 servings.

GOAT CHEESE SOUFFLÉS

Scant cup milk
1 shallot, finely chopped
1 bay leaf
6 black peppercorns
3 tablespoons butter
1/3 cup all-purpose flour
4 oz. goat cheese
3 eggs, separated
1 tablespoon chopped fresh chives
Salt and freshly ground pepper
2/3 cup whipping cream
1/4 cup coarsely grated Parmesan cheese
Mâche and hazelnuts, to garnish

Preheat oven to 350F (180C). Butter 6 (2/3-cup) ramekins. Put milk, shallot, bay leaf and peppercorns into a saucepan and bring slowly to a boil. Strain into a cup. Melt butter in a saucepan, add flour and cook, stirring, 2 minutes. Remove from heat and gradually stir in warm milk. Simmer 3 minutes. Crumble in goat cheese and stir until melted. Stir some sauce into egg yolks. Stir yolk mixture, chives, salt and pepper into sauce. Remove from heat. Whisk egg whites until holding soft peaks and fold into sauce.

Spoon into prepared ramekins. Stand dishes in a roasting pan and pour boiling water into pan to come one-third up sides of ramekins. Bake 15 to 20 minutes or until firm. Let cool. When ready to serve, preheat oven to 400F (205C). Run a knife round sides of ramekins and turn soufflés into a shallow ovenproof dish. Add cream, sprinkle with Parmesan cheese and bake 10 to 15 minutes or until golden. Garnish with mache and hazelnuts and serve.

Makes 6 servings.

ANCHOVY EGGS

1 (2-oz.) can anchovies in olive oil
6 eggs
Freshly ground pepper
2/3 cup whipping cream
2 tablespoons chopped fresh tarragon
1/2 cup fresh bread crumbs
Tarragon sprigs, to garnish

Preheat oven to 350F (180C). Butter 6 small ramekins. Drain anchovies, reserving oil, and coarsely chop. Divide anchovies among ramekins. Carefully break an egg into each ramekin; season with pepper.

Place ramekins in a roasting pan. Pour boiling water into pan to come halfway up sides of ramekins. Bake 6 minutes, or until eggs are just set. Spoon cream over eggs and sprinkle with chopped tarragon. Return to the oven 3 minutes.

Meanwhile, heat anchovy oil in a skillet. Add bread crumbs and cook, stirring, until crisp and golden. Place each ramekin on a serving plate and sprinkle with bread crumbs. Garnish with tarragon sprigs and serve.

Makes 6 servings.

— FETA & HERB POPOVERS —

1 tablespoon vegetable oil
Scant cup milk
1 tablespoon melted butter
2 eggs, beaten
3/4 cup all-purpose flour
2 teaspoons chopped fresh chives
2 teaspoons chopped fresh parsley
Salt and freshly ground pepper
4 oz. feta cheese, cut into 24 cubes
Flat-leaf parsley and chopped fresh chives, to
 garnish
MANGO SAUCE:
2 tablespoons mango chutney
3/4 cup regular plain yogurt

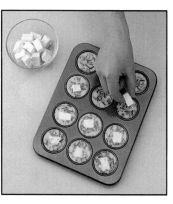

Preheat oven to 425F (220C). Brush cups in 2
(12-cup) mini muffin pans with oil and put
into the oven to heat. Stir milk and melted
butter into eggs. Sift flour into egg mixture
and whisk together to make a smooth batter.
Stir in chives, parsley, salt and pepper. Fill
each muffin cup with batter. Put a cube of
feta cheese in the center of each one and bake
20 to 25 minutes or until puffed and golden.

Meanwhile, make mango sauce. Put mango
chutney in a bowl, chopping any large pieces
of fruit. Stir in yogurt. Arrange popovers on
serving plates. Garnish with flat-leaf parsley
and chives and serve with mango sauce.

Makes 6 servings.

— PEARS WITH STILTON SAUCE —

3 large pears
1 tablespoon lemon juice
Chervil leaves, to garnish
STILTON SAUCE:
1/2 cup crème fraîche
2 tablespoons milk
3 oz. Stilton cheese
1 or 2 teaspoons fresh lemon juice
2 teaspoons poppy seeds
Salt and freshly ground pepper

To make sauce, put crème fraîche and milk
into a saucepan and heat gently. Crumble in
Stilton cheese and stir until melted.

Remove pan from heat, stir in lemon juice,
poppy seeds, salt and pepper and let cool.
Peel pears, if preferred. Cut each pear
lengthwise in half, keeping stalk intact if
possible. Using a small sharp knife, cut out
core. Brush lemon juice over cut surfaces.

Divide sauce among six serving plates. Slice
each pear half lengthwise and arrange on top
of sauce, in a fan shape. Garnish with chervil
leaves and serve.

Makes 6 servings.

—QUAIL EGGS IN FILO NESTS—

12 quail eggs
2 tablespoons butter, melted
2-1/2 sheets filo pastry, 16- x 12-inch rectangles
Tarragon leaves, to garnish
MUSHROOM DUXELLE:
12 oz. button mushrooms
2 tablespoons butter
2 shallots, finely chopped
Pinch of freshly grated nutmeg
Salt and freshly ground pepper
HOLLANDAISE SAUCE:
2 egg yolks
4 teaspoons lemon juice
1/2 cup butter
1/3 cup whipping cream
1 tablespoon chopped fresh tarragon

Preheat oven to 375F (190C). To make mushroom duxelle, finely chop mushrooms in a food processor or by hand. Heat butter in a saucepan. Add shallots and cook, stirring occasionally, 5 minutes or until soft. Add chopped mushrooms and cook over low heat, stirring occasionally, 5 minutes or until soft. Increase heat and cook until any liquid has evaporated. Season with nutmeg, salt and pepper and set aside.

Bring a saucepan of water to a boil. Place quail eggs into water and boil 1 minute. Put eggs into a colander and rinse with cold water. Carefully peel eggs. Heat some water in a saucepan, but do not boil. Put peeled eggs in the water to keep warm.

To make filo nests, turn 6 (3-inch) ramekins upside down and lightly brush all over with melted butter. Cut pastry into 18 (5-inch) squares. Brush a square with butter and press, butter side up, over an upturned ramekin. Butter a second square of filo and press over the first piece, arranging it at an angle so that the points form petals. Repeat with a third piece. Cover remaining ramekins in the same way. Bake 10 to 15 minutes or until crisp and golden. Carefully lift off pastry nests and place, right side up, on a baking sheet. Keep warm.

To make hollandaise sauce, put egg yolks in a heatproof bowl set over a pan of simmering water. Whisk in lemon juice and heat gently until warm. Melt butter and gradually whisk into egg yolks until mixture thickens. Stir in cream, tarragon, salt and pepper. Reheat mushroom duxelle.

Put a filo nest on each of six warmed serving plates. Divide mushroom duxelle among nests. Arrange two quail eggs in each nest. Spoon hollandaise sauce over eggs, garnish with tarragon leaves and serve at once.

Makes 6 servings.

Note: Filo pastry is available in different sizes, so you may have to adjust the number of sheets needed, depending on their size.

GORGONZOLA TARTLETS

6 green onions, chopped
4 oz. Gorgonzola cheese, crumbled
2 eggs, beaten
1 cup whipping cream
Salt and freshly ground pepper
SHORT CRUST PASTRY:
2-1/2 cups all-purpose flour
2/3 cup butter, diced
About 2-1/2 tablespoons cold water

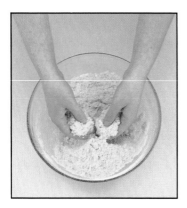

To make short crust pastry, sift flour into a bowl. Cut in butter until mixture resembles fine bread crumbs.

Stir in enough cold water to bind to a smooth dough. Wrap in plastic wrap and refrigerate 30 minutes. Preheat oven to 400F (205C). Thinly roll out pastry on a lightly floured surface. Cut circles to fit 6 (4-inch) loose-bottomed tartlet pans. Line pans with pastry, then press foil into pastry cases. Fill with dried beans and bake 15 minutes. Reduce oven temperature to 375F (190C).

Remove beans and foil, carefully remove pastry cases from pans and transfer to a baking sheet. Arrange green onions and cheese in pastry cases. Mix together eggs, cream, salt and pepper and pour into pastry cases. Bake 15 minutes or until set and golden. Serve warm.

Makes 6 servings.

SPINACH GNOCCHI

1 (1-lb.) package frozen leaf spinach
8 oz. ricotta cheese, drained
1 cup all-purpose flour
2 eggs, beaten
Pinch of freshly grated nutmeg
Salt and freshly ground pepper
24 cherry tomatoes
1/3 cup butter
2 oz. Parmesan cheese

Cook spinach as directed on package. Drain well and squeeze dry. Chop very finely in a food processor and let cool.

In a bowl, mix together spinach, ricotta, flour, eggs, nutmeg, salt and pepper. With floured hands, form mixture into small sausage shapes, about 3/4-inch long. Refrigerate at least 1 hour, until firm. Meanwhile, preheat oven to 400F (205C). Oil a roasting pan. Cut tomatoes in half and arrange, cut side up, in pan. Season with salt and pepper and roast 20 minutes.

Bring a large pan of salted water to a boil. Drop spinach gnocchi, a few at a time, into water. As they rise to the surface and float, remove with a slotted spoon. Drain thoroughly and keep warm while cooking remaining gnocchi. Heat butter in a saucepan. Add gnocchi and roasted tomatoes and stir gently to coat with butter. Divide among six warmed serving plates. Using a vegetable peeler, shave curls of Parmesan cheese over gnocchi and serve.

Makes 6 servings.

— FRUITY ROQUEFORT PARCELS —

1 ripe mango
4 oz. Roquefort cheese
1 teaspoon lime juice
Freshly ground pepper
8 sheets filo pastry, 12- x 8-inch rectangles
1/4 cup butter, melted
Strips of lime zest and mint leaves, to garnish
CUCUMBER SALSA:
1/2 cucumber, peeled, seeded and diced
Grated zest of 1 lime
1 teaspoon fresh lime juice
1 teaspoon chopped fresh mint

Peel mango, cut flesh away from pit and cut flesh into small cubes.

Cut Roquefort cheese into small cubes. Mix together mango, cheese, lime juice and pepper. Lightly brush a sheet of filo pastry with melted butter. Layer three more sheets on top, brushing each one with butter. Layer remaining four sheets in the same way. Cut each stack of pastry into 3 (4-inch-wide) strips. Brush a baking sheet with butter. Preheat oven to 425F (220C).

Place a spoonful of mango filling in one corner of a strip and diagonally fold over the corner. Continue folding over the filled corner of pastry to form a triangular parcel. Place on baking sheet and brush lightly with butter. Repeat with remaining pastry and filling. Bake 7 to 10 minutes or until golden brown. To make cucumber salsa, mix together cucumber, lime zest and juice and mint. Garnish triangles with lime zest and mint leaves and serve with cucumber salsa.

Makes 6 servings.

DEEP-FRIED BRIE

6 oz. firm Brie, chilled
2 eggs
Salt and freshly ground pepper
1-1/2 cups fresh bread crumbs
Sunflower oil for deep-frying
Strips of orange zest, to garnish
CRANBERRY RELISH:
2 tablespoons sunflower oil
1 onion, finely chopped
1 Golden Delicious apple, peeled, cored and
   chopped
6 oz. cranberries
Grated zest and juice of 1 orange
1 cinnamon stick
1/3 cup light brown sugar

Cut cheese into six wedges and trim off rind.

To make cranberry relish, heat oil in a saucepan, add onion and cook, stirring occasionally, 5 minutes or until soft. Add apple, cranberries, orange zest and juice, cinnamon stick and sugar. Simmer until sugar has dissolved, then bring to a boil. Simmer 10 to 15 minutes or until cranberries have popped and softened. In a shallow dish, beat eggs with salt and pepper. Spread bread crumbs in another dish.

Dip cheese wedges into egg and then into bread crumbs, making sure cheese is completely coated. Heat oil in a deep-fat fryer to 190C (375F), or until a cube of bread browns in 40 seconds. Fry cheese portions, three at a time, 2 minutes or until golden and crisp. Drain on paper towels and keep warm while frying remaining wedges. Garnish with orange zest and serve at once with cranberry relish.

Makes 6 servings.

— BAKED EGGPLANT LAYERS —

2 large eggplant
Salt
2 red bell peppers, peeled (page 30)
1/3 cup olive oil
10 oz. mozzarella cheese, thinly sliced
Oregano leaves, to garnish
TOMATO SAUCE:
2 tablespoons olive oil
2 garlic cloves, crushed
1-1/2 lbs. plum tomatoes, peeled and chopped
2 teaspoons chopped fresh oregano
Salt and freshly ground pepper

Cut eggplant into 1/2-inch-thick slices. Place in a colander, sprinkle generously with salt and leave 1 hour. Cut bell peppers into thin strips.

To make tomato sauce, heat olive oil in a skillet. Add garlic and cook a few minutes or until soft. Add tomatoes, oregano, salt and pepper and cook over low heat, stirring, 2 minutes, without allowing tomatoes to lose their texture. Keep warm.

Preheat broiler. Rinse eggplant well, drain and dry thoroughly with paper towels. Arrange on a rack in a baking pan. Brush with 1/4 cup of the olive oil and broil on both sides until soft and beginning to brown.

Preheat oven to 350F (180C). Place half the eggplant slices on a baking sheet. Arrange mozzarella slices on top, cutting to fit if necessary. Top with half the pepper strips. Place remaining eggplant slices on top. Drizzle with remaining olive oil.

Bake 3 to 5 minutes or until heated through, but do not allow cheese to melt. Arrange remaining strips of bell pepper on top, garnish with oregano leaves and serve with tomato sauce.

Makes 6 servings.

—WARM GOAT CHEESE SALAD—

6 slices French bread
1 garlic clove, halved
1 (5-inch) log goat cheese
7 oz. mixed salad greens
1/2 cup walnuts, coarsely chopped
WALNUT DRESSING:
1 tablespoon balsamic vinegar
1/4 cup olive oil
2 tablespoons walnut oil
Salt and freshly ground pepper

To make dressing, put vinegar, olive oil, walnut oil, salt and pepper in a bowl and whisk together. Set aside.

Preheat broiler. Toast bread slices lightly on both sides. Rub one side of each slice with cut face of garlic clove. Cut cheese into 6 slices and place a slice on garlic side of each toast slice. Broil 4 or 5 minutes or until slightly browned but not melting.

Put salad greens in a bowl, add dressing and toss. Arrange salad on serving plates. Place cheese toasts on salad, sprinkle with walnuts and serve immediately.

Makes 6 servings.

– CHICKEN & APRICOT TERRINE –

1 lb. ground chicken
8 oz. ground pork
3 oz. dried apricots, coarsely chopped
1 garlic clove, crushed
2/3 cup dry white wine
2 tablespoons chopped fresh mint
1/2 teaspoon ground cinnamon
Salt and freshly ground pepper
Mint leaves, to garnish
APRICOT VINAIGRETTE:
1 oz. dried apricots
2 teaspoons chopped fresh mint leaves
4 teaspoons white wine vinegar
1/3 cup olive oil

Preheat oven to 350F (180C). In a bowl, mix together ground chicken and ground pork. Add apricots, garlic, wine, mint, cinnamon, salt and pepper and mix well. Spoon into a 3-3/4-cup terrine or loaf pan. Cover tightly with foil and put into a roasting pan. Pour boiling water into roasting pan to come halfway up sides of terrine. Bake 1 hour, or until juices run clear. Let cool. Remove from pan, wrap in foil and refrigerate overnight.

To make vinaigrette, put apricots in a small saucepan and add enough water to cover. Bring to a boil, reduce heat and simmer 10 to 15 minutes or until soft. Drain apricots and put into a blender or food processor with mint, vinegar, oil, salt and pepper. Process until smooth. Allow terrine to come to room temperature before serving. Slice terrine, garnish with mint leaves and serve with vinaigrette.

Makes 6 servings.

PROSCIUTTO BASKETS

2 sheets filo pastry, 16- x 12-inch rectangles
2 tablespoons butter, melted
1 tablespoon olive oil
1 red onion, finely chopped
1 teaspoon sugar
5 oz. prosciutto, coarsely chopped
10 sun-dried tomatoes, coarsely chopped
7 oz. salad greens
Basil leaves, to garnish
DRESSING:
1/4 cup olive oil
2 teaspoons white wine vinegar
Salt and freshly ground pepper

Preheat oven to 375F (190C). Cut filo pastry into 24 (4-inch) squares.

Lightly brush a 12-cup muffin pan with butter. Brush 12 sheets of pastry with butter. Line each cup with a square of pastry. Brush remaining sheets of pastry with melted butter and place on top, arranging them so that the points are like petals. Bake 10 minutes or until golden. Keep warm. Heat oil in a saucepan, add onion and cook, stirring occasionally, 5 minutes, until soft. Add sugar and cook 3 minutes. Stir in prosciutto and sun-dried tomatoes. Heat over low heat to warm through.

To make dressing, put olive oil, wine vinegar, salt and pepper in a large bowl and whisk together. Add salad greens and toss well. Arrange salad on six serving plates. Fill tartlet cases with prosciutto mixture. Arrange on serving plates, garnish with basil leaves and serve.

Makes 6 servings.

—— PISTACHIO LIVER PÂTÉ ——

1/2 cup butter
2 shallots, finely chopped
2 garlic cloves, crushed
1-1/2 lbs. chicken livers, trimmed
2 tablespoons sherry
1 (8-oz.) package low-fat cream cheese
Salt and freshly ground pepper
1 teaspoon chopped fresh thyme
1/3 cup pistachio nuts, coarsely chopped
Thyme leaves, to garnish
Bread slices, toasted, to serve

Melt butter in a large skillet, add shallots and garlic and cook 5 minutes, stirring occasionally, until soft.

Rinse chicken livers, dry with paper towels and coarsely chop. Add to skillet and cook over medium to high heat, stirring, 5 minutes, or until livers are browned outside and still slightly pink inside. Cool slightly, then put into a blender or food processor with sherry, cream cheese, salt and pepper and process until well blended. Transfer to a bowl and stir in thyme and nuts. Refrigerate overnight.

Allow pâté to come to room temperature before serving. Shape pâté into ovals using two spoons and put 2 or 3 ovals on each serving plate. Garnish with thyme leaves and serve with toasted bread.

Makes 6 to 8 servings.

—CARIBBEAN TURKEY MOUSSE—

12 oz. ground turkey
1 small mango, peeled and coarsely chopped
2 egg whites and 1 egg, beaten
Grated zest and juice of 1 lime
3/4-inch piece ginger root, peeled and grated
Salt and freshly ground pepper
1/2 cup whipping cream
Strips of lime zest and mint leaves, to garnish
MANGO SALSA:
1 large mango, chopped
Juice of 1 lime
1 fresh red chile, cored, seeded and finely chopped
1 small red onion, finely chopped
Salt and freshly ground pepper
2 tablespoons chopped fresh mint

Put ground turkey into a blender or food processor. Add mango, egg whites and egg, lime zest and juice and ginger root. Process until just smooth, then season with salt and pepper. With motor running, gradually add cream until just blended. Do not over process. Transfer mixture to a bowl, cover and refrigerate 30 minutes. Preheat oven to 325F (165C). Lightly grease 6 (3-inch) ramekins.

Divide turkey mixture among ramekins. Smooth top and cover each one with foil. Place in a roasting pan and pour in boiling water to come halfway up sides of ramekins. Bake 20 to 25 minutes or until a skewer inserted in center comes out clean. To make salsa, mix together mango, lime juice, chile, onion, mint, salt and pepper. Refrigerate until required. Turn mousses onto serving plates, garnish and serve hot or cold with salsa.

Makes 6 servings.

CARPACCIO

1 (1-lb.) piece beef fillet
6 oz. arugula leaves
Juice of 2 lemons
1/2 cup extra-virgin olive oil
Freshly ground pepper
3 oz. Parmesan cheese
Capers, to garnish

Wrap beef fillet tightly in foil, seal well and freeze 1 or 2 hours or until just firm but not frozen solid. Wash and dry arugula leaves and remove any thick stalks. Arrange arugula leaves on serving plates.

Unwrap fillet and use a large sharp knife to cut into wafer-thin slices. Arrange beef slices, slightly overlapping, in center of plates.

Drizzle lemon juice and olive oil over beef and season with pepper. Using a vegetable peeler, shave curls of Parmesan cheese over beef. Garnish with capers and serve immediately.

Makes 6 servings.

Note: A good quality olive oil is essential to the success of this dish.

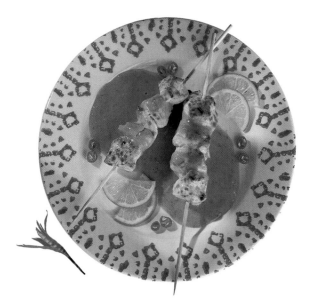

CHICKEN SATAY

Juice of 1 lime
1 stalk lemon grass, finely chopped
1 garlic clove, finely chopped
2 tablespoons sunflower oil
1 teaspoon ground coriander
1 lb. boneless, skinless chicken breasts
Lime slices and chile rings, to garnish
PEANUT SAUCE:
2 oz. smooth peanut butter
2/3 cup coconut milk
2 teaspoons Thai red curry paste
1 tablespoon Thai fish sauce
1 tablespoon light brown sugar

Mix together lime juice, lemon grass, garlic, sunflower oil and ground coriander.

Cut chicken into 3/4-inch cubes and add to marinade. Turn to coat, cover and leave to marinate at least 1 hour. Meanwhile, make peanut sauce. Mix together peanut butter, coconut milk, red curry paste, fish sauce and sugar and set aside. Soak twelve bamboo skewers in water 30 minutes.

Preheat broiler. Thread chicken onto skewers. Broil, turning frequently, 8 to 10 minutes or until cooked through and browned on the outside. Garnish with lime slices and chile rings and serve with peanut sauce.

Makes 6 servings.

—— PROSCIUTTO WITH FRUIT ——

1 large mango
4 figs
6 physalis
6 lychees
Juice of 1/2 lime
18 slices prosciutto
Freshly ground pepper
1 pomegranate

Peel mango and cut down either side of the narrow pit, to remove flesh. Cut away narrow band of flesh still attached to pit. Thinly slice mango flesh.

Cut figs into wedges. Peel back papery skin from fruit of physalis. Peel lychees. Put all fruits in a bowl and sprinkle with lime juice.

Arrange prosciutto and fruit on serving plates. Season with pepper. Cut pomegranate in half and scoop out seeds. Scatter seeds over prosciutto and fruit and serve.

Makes 6 servings.

Variation: Other exotic fruit may be used with prosciutto, such as melon, guava, papaya or prickly pear.

—CHICKEN LIVERS & GRAPES—

1 lb. chicken livers, trimmed
Salt and freshly ground pepper
4 teaspoons olive oil
2 shallots, finely chopped
2 garlic cloves, crushed
2 tablespoons dry sherry
4 oz. seedless green grapes, halved
1 teaspoon chopped fresh rosemary
6 slices brioche
Rosemary sprigs, to garnish

Rinse chicken livers and dry with paper towels. Cut into even-size pieces. Season with salt and pepper.

Heat oil in a large skillet. Add shallots and garlic and cook, stirring occasionally, 5 minutes or until soft. Add chicken livers and cook over medium to high heat, stirring, 5 minutes or until browned on the outside and still slightly pink inside.

Add sherry, grapes and rosemary and cook, stirring, until grapes are heated through. Meanwhile, lightly toast brioche slices. Put toasted brioche on warmed serving plates and top with chicken liver mixture. Garnish with rosemary sprigs and serve immediately.

Makes 6 servings.

TURKEY TACOS

3 tomatoes
1/4 head iceberg lettuce
2 tablespoons sunflower oil
1 onion, finely chopped
1 garlic clove, crushed
1 fresh green chile, cored, seeded and finely
   chopped
1/2 cup chicken stock
8 oz. cooked turkey, shredded
1 tablespoon chopped fresh cilantro
Salt
6 taco shells
2/3 cup sour cream

Finely chop tomatoes and set aside. Finely shred lettuce and set aside.

Preheat oven to 350F (180C). Heat oil in a skillet, add onion, garlic and chile and cook, stirring occasionally, 5 minutes, until soft. Add stock and boil 5 minutes or until nearly all liquid has evaporated. Add turkey and cook 2 minutes. Stir in cilantro and salt and keep warm.

Arrange taco shells on a baking sheet and heat in the oven 2 or 3 minutes. Divide shredded lettuce among serving plates. Spoon turkey mixture into hot shells and place on top of lettuce. Serve with diced tomato and a spoonful of sour cream.

Makes 6 servings.

── INDONESIAN SPARE RIBS ──

3 lb. pork spareribs, cut into 1 rib pieces
1/4 cup sunflower oil
Chopped green onions and diced red bell pepper, to
    garnish
MARINADE:
1-inch piece ginger root, peeled and grated
2 garlic cloves, finely chopped
1 fresh red chile, cored, seeded and finely chopped
1/3 cup soy sauce
Juice of 1 lemon
2 tablespoons sunflower oil
2 tablespoons honey
1 teaspoon five-spice powder

Mix together all marinade ingredients.

Put spareribs into a shallow, nonmetallic dish, add marinade and turn ribs to coat thoroughly. Cover and refrigerate 2 or 3 hours, turning occasionally. Remove ribs from marinade, reserving marinade, and dry ribs with paper towels. Heat oil in a wok or large skillet, add ribs and cook, in batches, 2 or 3 minutes, turning, until browned.

Pour off most of oil, return ribs to pan and add marinade and enough water to cover. Bring to a boil, reduce heat, cover and simmer, stirring occasionally, 1 hour, or until meat is tender. Boil rapidly to reduce cooking liquid to a thick sauce. Arrange ribs and sauce on warmed serving plates. Garnish with chopped green onions and diced red bell pepper and serve.

Makes 6 servings.

SAFFRON MUSSELS

6 lbs. mussels
3 tablespoons unsweetened apple juice
SAFFRON SAUCE:
2 tablespoons olive oil
3 shallots, finely chopped
1 garlic clove, crushed
3/4 cup unsweetened apple juice
Large pinch of saffron strands
Freshly ground pepper
2 tablespoons butter
2 tablespoons chopped fresh parsley

Discard broken mussels and any which do not close when tapped sharply. Scrape off any barnacles, remove 'beards' and scrub.

To make sauce, heat olive oil in a saucepan. Add shallots and garlic and cook, stirring occasionally, 5 minutes or until soft. Set aside. Put mussels and apple juice into a large saucepan. Bring to a boil, cover tightly and cook over high heat, shaking pan occasionally, 4 or 5 minutes or until mussels have opened.

Remove mussels with a slotted spoon, discarding any that have not opened. Transfer to warmed serving plates and keep warm. Line a strainer with cheesecloth, place over a measuring cup and strain cooking liquid. Add 2/3 cup cooking liquid to shallots and garlic. Add apple juice, saffron and pepper. Bring to a boil and boil until reduced by one-third. Whisk in butter. Stir in parsley, pour over mussels and serve.

Makes 6 servings.

—MEDITERRANEAN SCALLOPS—

1-1/2 lbs. shelled scallops
3 tablespoons olive oil
1 garlic clove, crushed
4 teaspoons fresh thyme leaves
Salt and freshly ground pepper
MEDITERRANEAN VEGETABLES:
2 tablespoons olive oil
1 shallot, finely chopped
1 garlic clove, crushed
1 eggplant, diced
2 zucchini, diced
1 red and 1 yellow bell pepper, diced
Juice of 1/2 lemon
1 tablespoon chopped fresh oregano

Rinse scallops, dry with paper towels and cut in half crosswise. Place in a bowl with oil, garlic, thyme, salt and pepper. Mix well, cover and refrigerate. To prepare vegetables, heat oil in a skillet, add shallots and garlic and cook, stirring occasionally, 5 minutes or until soft. Add eggplant, zucchini and bell peppers and stir-fry over high heat until softened but still retaining some texture. Keep warm.

Heat a large heavy skillet. Add scallops in one layer and cook 1 minute. Turn and cook other side 1 minute. Add lemon juice, oregano, salt and pepper to vegetables. Arrange vegetables in scallop shells, place scallops on top and serve.

Makes 6 servings.

Note: If the scallops have their coral with them you can use that too.

— SHRIMP & LETTUCE ROLLS —

2 heads iceberg lettuces
1 tablespoon olive oil
1 bunch of green onions, chopped
1 garlic clove, crushed
1 red bell pepper, diced
8 oz. cooked, peeled medium shrimp
4 teaspoons chopped fresh chives
Salt and freshly ground pepper
1-1/4 cups dry white wine
1-1/4 cups fish stock
1/2 cup butter, diced
1 teaspoon pink peppercorns
Chives and red bell pepper strips, to garnish

Separate 12 large leaves from lettuces and wash. Bring a large pan of water to a boil, add lettuce leaves and blanch 30 seconds. Drain and plunge into a bowl of cold water. Spread on a kitchen towel and leave to drain. Heat oil in a saucepan, add green onions, garlic and bell pepper and cook, stirring occasionally, 3 minutes. Add shrimp, half the chives, salt and pepper.

Divide filling among lettuce leaves and wrap up to form rolls. Put wine and stock in a saucepan. Bring to a boil and boil rapidly until reduced by half. Add rolls and simmer to warm through. Remove with a slotted spoon, transfer to warmed serving plates and keep warm. Whisk butter into sauce, a little at a time, until thickened. Stir in remaining chives and pink peppercorns. Pour around rolls, garnish with chives and bell pepper strips and serve.

Makes 6 servings.

THAI SQUID SALAD

1-3/4 lbs. fresh squid
Juice of 1 lime
2 tablespoons Thai fish sauce
1 fresh red chile, cored, seeded and finely chopped
1 garlic clove, crushed
1-inch piece ginger root, peeled and grated
2 stalks lemon grass, thinly sliced
6 green onions, thinly sliced
2 tablespoons chopped fresh cilantro
10 mint leaves, coarsely chopped
7 oz. salad greens
Chile rings, to garnish

To clean squid, pull head and tentacles away from body pouch and discard.

Remove viscera and discard. Remove transparent pen from body. Remove any purple skin from body. Rinse body pouch thoroughly and slit open. Score inside of body in a crisscross pattern, then cut into 2- x 1/2-inch strips. Bring a saucepan of water to a boil.

Add squid and simmer 1 minute, until opaque. Drain and put into a bowl. Add lime juice, fish sauce, chile, garlic, ginger root, lemon grass and green onions. Cover and marinate 1 hour or longer if refrigerated. Stir in cilantro and mint. Arrange salad greens on serving plates, top with squid mixture, garnish with chile rings and serve.

Makes 6 servings.

SALMON MOUSSE

12 oz. skinless salmon fillet
1/2 cup cream cheese
1/2 cup regular plain yogurt
2 eggs, beaten
Salt and freshly ground pepper
2 teaspoons fresh lemon juice
1 tablespoon chopped fresh dill
Dill sprigs, to garnish
SORREL SAUCE:
1 tablespoon butter
4 oz. sorrel, very finely chopped
2/3 cup whipping cream

Preheat oven to 325F (165C). Lightly oil 6 (1/2-cup) cup-shaped molds. Cut salmon into cubes and put into a blender or food processor with cream cheese, yogurt, eggs, salt and pepper. Process until smooth. Add lemon juice and dill and process briefly. Spoon mixture into prepared molds, then place in a roasting pan. Pour in boiling water to come one-third of the way up sides of molds. Cover each one with foil and bake about 20 minutes or until a skewer inserted in center comes out clean.

To make sauce, melt butter in a saucepan over medium heat, add sorrel and cook, stirring, 2 or 3 minutes or until softened. Stir in cream, salt and pepper, bring to a boil, reduce heat and simmer 2 or 3 minutes, to thicken slightly. Turn each mousse onto a warmed serving plate, pour a little sorrel sauce around mousse, garnish with dill sprigs and serve.

Makes 6 servings.

SEAFOOD DIAMONDS

12 oz. puff pastry, thawed if frozen
1 egg, beaten
8 oz. smoked haddock fillet
8 oz. monkfish fillet
8 oz. leeks
2 tablespoons butter
2 teaspoons all-purpose flour
2/3 cup dry white wine
Large pinch of saffron strands
2 teaspoons lemon juice
Salt and freshly ground pepper
1/4 cup whipping cream
4 oz. cooked, peeled large shrimp
Salad greens, to garnish

Preheat oven to 425F (220C). Roll out pastry on a lightly floured surface until 1/8 inch thick. Cut out 12 diamonds and arrange on a baking sheet. Brush pastry with beaten egg. Bake 10 minutes or until puffed and golden brown. Split each diamond in half and keep warm.

Meanwhile, put smoked haddock in a saucepan, cover with cold water, bring to a boil, reduce heat and simmer 5 minutes or until just cooked. Remove haddock, reserving cooking liquid. Flake fish into a bowl, discarding skin. Cut monkfish into 3/4-inch cubes. Add monkfish to cooking liquid and cook 5 minutes. Remove with a slotted spoon, reserving cooking liquid, and add monkfish to bowl.

Cut leeks lengthwise in half and thinly slice. Melt butter in a saucepan, add leeks and cook, stirring occasionally, 5 to 10 minutes or until soft. Stir in flour and cook, stirring, 1 minute. Stir in 2/3 cup reserved fish cooking liquid, bring to a boil, reduce heat and simmer 2 minutes.

Put wine and saffron into a small saucepan, bring to a boil and boil rapidly until reduced to 2 tablespoons. Strain into leek sauce. Stir in lemon juice, salt and pepper. Add cream, haddock, monkfish and shrimp and heat to warm through.

Arrange bottom halves of two pastry diamonds on each warmed serving plate. Spoon fish mixture over pastry and top with glazed pastry lids. Garnish and serve.

Makes 6 servings.

SHRIMP & FETA PURSES

4 oz. cooked, peeled large shrimp
8 oz. feta cheese
1 garlic clove, crushed
2 tablespoons chopped fresh dill
Grated zest of 1 lime
Salt and freshly ground pepper
3 sheets filo pastry, 16- x 12-inch rectangles
2 tablespoons butter, melted
Dill sprigs and lime wedges, to garnish
DILL SAUCE:
2/3 cup sour cream
2/3 cup whipping cream, whipped
1 teaspoon fresh lime juice
2 teaspoons chopped fresh dill

Preheat oven to 400F (205C). Coarsely chop shrimp and put into a bowl. Crumble in feta cheese, then add garlic, dill, lime zest, salt and pepper. Cut each sheet of filo pastry into 12 squares. Lightly brush each square with melted butter. Lay two squares on top of one another, arranging points at an angle like petals. Put a teaspoon of shrimp filling in center and pull up pastry, pinching together above filling to make a purse. Repeat to make 18 purses.

Brush a baking sheet with melted butter. Place purses on baking sheet, brush with a little melted butter and bake 10 to 15 minutes or until golden. Meanwhile, make sauce. In a bowl, mix together sour cream, whipped cream, lime juice, dill, salt and pepper. Garnish purses with dill sprigs and lime wedges and serve with sauce.

Makes 6 servings.

—SMOKED SALMON MOUSSE—

1-1/4 lbs. thinly sliced smoked salmon
5 oz. cream cheese, softened
2/3 cup regular plain yogurt
Juice of 1/2 lemon
Salt and freshly ground pepper
Pinch of cayenne pepper
Tarragon sprigs, to garnish
CUCUMBER VINAIGRETTE:
1/3 cup light olive oil
Juice of 1/2 lemon
1 tablespoon chopped fresh tarragon
1/8 cucumber, seeded and finely diced

Line 6 (1/2-cup) ramekins with plastic wrap. Line with half the smoked salmon.

Put remaining smoked salmon into a blender or food processor with cream cheese, yogurt, lemon juice, salt and cayenne. Process until smooth. Spoon into lined ramekins, cover and refrigerate at least 4 hours.

To make vinaigrette, whisk together oil and lemon juice. Stir in tarragon, cucumber, salt and pepper. Turn each mousse out onto a serving plate and remove plastic wrap. Garnish with tarragon sprigs and serve with cucumber vinaigrette.

Makes 6 servings.

—FISH & WATERCRESS TERRINE—

1/4 cucumber, very thinly sliced
1 lb. sole fillets
1/3 cup dry white wine
1 tablespoon fresh lemon juice
2 bay leaves
4 black peppercorns
1 tablespoon powdered gelatin
1 (8-oz.) cream cheese, softened
4 oz. watercress, stalks removed
1/2 cup whipping cream
Salt and freshly ground pepper
4 oz. thinly sliced smoked salmon
Lemon slices, lemon zest and sprigs of watercress, to
  garnish
WATERCRESS SAUCE:
1 oz. watercress, stalks removed
1 cup crème fraîche
1 tablespoon lemon juice

Spread cucumber slices on paper towels, sprinkle with salt and leave to drain. Line a 4-1/2-cup terrine or loaf pan with plastic wrap. Place sole in a saucepan. Add wine, 1/3 cup water, lemon juice, bay leaves and peppercorns. Bring slowly to a boil, reduce heat, cover and simmer 10 minutes or until fish flakes easily. Remove fish, reserving cooking liquid and flake fish, discarding skin.

Pour 1/3 cup warm water into a large bowl, sprinkle with gelatin and leave 5 minutes or until absorbed. Bring fish cooking liquid to a boil and boil rapidly until reduced by half. Strain into bowl of gelatin and stir until gelatin has dissolved.

Put sole into a blender or food processor with cream cheese and process until blended. With motor running, pour gelatin mixture onto fish mixture and blend. Remove three-quarters of mixture, transfer to a bowl and set aside. Add watercress to blender and process briefly. Transfer to a bowl. Lightly whip cream. Fold just under half of cream into watercress mixture and remainder into white fish mixture.

Season both with salt and pepper. Dry cucumber with paper towels and arrange half in bottom of terrine. Spread half white fish mixture over bottom of pan and cover with half smoked salmon. Cover with watercress mixture and then the remaining smoked salmon. Top with remaining white fish mixture. Cover with remaining cucumber slices. Cover pan and refrigerate 4 hours.

To make sauce, put watercress, crème fraîche, lemon juice, salt and pepper in a blender or food processor and process until smooth. Turn out terrine and slice. Garnish and serve with sauce.

Makes 6 to 8 servings.

—MUSSEL & FENNEL TARTLETS—

1 recipe short crust pastry (page 82)
3 lbs. mussels, trimmed (page 99)
1/2 cup dry white wine
2 tablespoons butter
1 bunch of green onions, finely chopped
1 garlic clove, crushed
1 large fennel bulb, halved and thinly sliced
2 teaspoons fresh lemon juice
1/4 cup whipping cream
Salt and freshly ground pepper
Fennel leaves, to garnish

Preheat oven to 400F (205C). Roll out pastry on a lightly floured surface and use to line 6 (4-inch) loose-bottomed tartlet pans. Line with foil.

Fill with dried beans and bake 10 minutes. Remove foil and beans and bake 2 or 3 minutes or until pastry is cooked and golden. Keep warm. Put mussels into a large saucepan with 2 tablespoons of the wine. Bring to a boil, cover tightly and cook over high heat, shaking pan occasionally, 4 or 5 minutes or until mussels open. Drain, reserving cooking liquid and discarding any mussels that have not opened. Remove mussels from shells, discarding shells, and keep warm.

Melt butter in a saucepan. Add green onions, garlic and fennel and cook, stirring occasionally, 5 minutes or until soft. Add remaining white wine, lemon juice and 1/3 cup mussel cooking liquid. Simmer until reduced by half. Add cream and boil for a few minutes or until thickened. Season with salt and pepper. Add mussels to fennel mixture and heat gently to warm through. Spoon into pastry cases. Garnish with fennel and serve.

Makes 6 servings.

MONKFISH TEMPURA

1 lb. monkfish fillets
Sunflower oil for deep-frying
BATTER:
1 cup all-purpose flour
1 egg, beaten
1 egg yolk
3/4 cup ice water
BELL PEPPER SALSA:
1/2 red onion, finely diced
1 fresh green chile, cored, seeded and chopped
1 red bell pepper, finely diced
2 tablespoons fresh lemon juice
1 tablespoon chopped fresh parsley
Salt

Mix together ingredients for salsa in a small bowl. Cover and refrigerate until required.

Cut monkfish into strips. To make batter, sift flour into a bowl and whisk in egg, egg yolk and ice water. Heat 2 inches oil in a pan or wok.

Dip monkfish strips into batter and fry, in batches, until crisp and pale golden. Drain on paper towels and keep warm while cooking remaining fish. Divide among serving plates and serve with salsa.

Makes 6 servings.

THAI CRAB CAKES

2 tablespoons butter
1/4 cup all-purpose flour
2/3 cup milk
12 oz. crabmeat
2 teaspoons chopped fresh cilantro
2-1/2 cups fresh bread crumbs
Grated zest of 1/2 lime
2 teaspoons fresh lime juice
4 green onions, finely chopped
1 teaspoon Thai green curry paste
2 teaspoons Thai fish sauce
1 egg, beaten
1/3 cup sunflower oil
Lime slices and cilantro leaves, to garnish

Melt butter in a saucepan. Add flour and cook, stirring, 1 minute. Remove from heat and gradually stir in milk. Simmer, stirring, 2 or 3 minutes or until thickened. Remove from heat. Stir in crab, cilantro, 1/2 cup of the bread crumbs, lime zest and juice, green onions, curry paste and fish sauce. Let cool. Spread mixture into a round and cut into 12 wedges. With floured hands, shape each wedge into a round cake.

Put remaining bread crumbs on a plate and put beaten egg in a shallow dish. Dip each crab cake in beaten egg and then in bread crumbs, to coat thoroughly. Refrigerate 15 minutes. Heat oil in a skillet and fry crab cakes 3 or 4 minutes on each side, until crisp and golden. Garnish with lime slices and cilantro leaves and serve.

Makes 6 servings.

CHICKEN & CRAB ROLLS

12 spring roll wrappers
8 oz. cooked chicken, finely chopped
4 oz. crabmeat
4 green onions, finely chopped
1 small carrot, grated
2 teaspoons Thai fish sauce
2 teaspoons soy sauce
1 garlic clove, crushed
1 celery stalk, finely diced
12 small, crisp lettuce leaves
Sunflower oil for deep-frying
Green onion flowers, to garnish

Place spring roll wrappers between two clean damp towels, to soften.

In a bowl, mix together chicken, crab, green onions, carrot, fish sauce, soy sauce, garlic and celery. Place a lettuce leaf in middle of each spring roll wrapper. Place a spoonful of chicken mixture on each lettuce leaf. Fold over three sides of wrapper to enclose filling. Roll up firmly.

Heat oil in a wok or deep-fat fryer to 190C (375F), or until a cube of bread browns in 40 seconds. Add rolls and fry, in batches, 3 minutes, or until crisp and golden. Drain on paper towels. Garnish with green onion flowers and serve with chile dipping sauce.

Makes 6 servings.

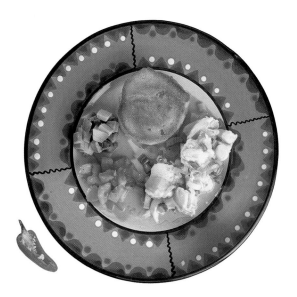

MEXICAN SEVICHE

1 lb. skinless cod fillets
1 bunch green onions, thinly sliced
Juice of 1 orange and 5 limes
3 tablespoons olive oil
1 fresh green chile, cored, seeded and chopped
Salt
2 tomatoes
1 avocado
CORNMEAL PANCAKES:
1/2 cup self-rising flour
1/3 cup cornmeal
1 teaspoon baking powder
1/2 fresh red chile, cored, seeded and chopped
1 egg, beaten
1/2 cup milk
Sunflower oil for frying

Cut fish into bite-size pieces and put into a nonmetallic dish with green onions and orange and lime juice. Mix well, cover and refrigerate 3 hours or until fish becomes opaque and looks cooked. Stir in olive oil, chile and 1/2 teaspoon salt, cover and refrigerate 1 hour. To make pancakes, put flour, cornmeal, baking powder, 1/2 teaspoon salt and chile into a bowl. Mix together egg and milk, add to dry ingredients and mix to form a smooth batter.

Heat a little oil in a skillet. Drop spoonfuls of batter onto pan to make 6 small pancakes and cook 2 or 3 minutes on each side, until cooked through and golden brown. Keep warm. Halve avocado lengthwise, remove pit and peel. Dice avocado flesh and tomatoes. Serve seviche with pancakes, avocado and tomatoes.

Makes 6 servings.

— CRAB WITH TOMATO SALSA —

12 to 18 cooked crab claws
TOMATO SALSA:
1 lb. tomatoes, peeled
1/2 small red onion, finely chopped
3 green onions, finely chopped
1 fresh green chile, cored, seeded and finely
  chopped
2 tablespoons chopped fresh cilantro
2 teaspoons fresh lemon juice
Salt and freshly ground pepper
CORN CHIPS:
6 corn tortillas
Olive oil for brushing

Preheat oven to 400F (205C). To make tomato salsa, finely dice tomatoes.

Mix together tomatoes, red onion, green onions, chile, cilantro, lemon juice, salt and pepper. Refrigerate until required.

To make corn chips, brush tortillas with oil and cut into quarters. Arrange in a single layer on a baking sheet. Bake 10 minutes or until golden and crisp. Serve crab claws with tomato salsa and corn chips.

Makes 6 servings.

—BROILED STUFFED MUSSELS—

6 lbs. mussels, trimmed (page 99)
1/4 cup dry white wine
1/2 cup butter, softened
1 garlic clove, crushed
2 shallots, very finely chopped
1/4 cup pesto
Salt and freshly ground pepper
1/2 cup fresh bread crumbs
1/4 cup grated Parmesan cheese
Basil leaves, to garnish

Put mussels and wine into a large saucepan. Bring to a boil, cover tightly and cook over high heat, shaking pan occasionally, 4 or 5 minutes or until mussels open.

Line a baking sheet with crumpled foil. Drain mussels, discarding any that remain closed. Remove top shell from each mussel and arrange lower shells on baking sheet. In a bowl, mix together butter, garlic, shallots, pesto, salt and pepper.

Preheat broiler. Spoon a little butter mixture onto each mussel in shells. In a bowl, mix together bread crumbs and Parmesan cheese and sprinkle over mussels. Broil 5 minutes or until bubbling and golden. Garnish with basil leaves and serve immediately.

Makes 6 servings.

Variation: This dish can also be made with clams.

SEARED TUNA

1 (1-1/4-lb.) piece tuna steak
1 tablespoon soy sauce
2 tablespoons mixed peppercorns, crushed
TOMATO & ANCHOVY SALSA:
4 tomatoes, seeded and diced
1 (2-oz.) can anchovies in olive oil
1 garlic clove, crushed
2 tablespoons olive oil
2 tablespoons chopped fresh parsley
Salt and freshly ground pepper

Brush tuna with soy sauce. Press crushed peppercorns all over tuna.

Heat a heavy skillet or ridged broiler pan until very hot, then brush with oil. Add tuna and cook over high heat 2 minutes per side. Let cool slightly, then wrap tightly and refrigerate until required.

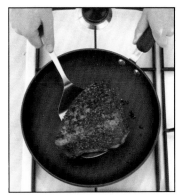

To make salsa, put tomatoes into a bowl. Drain anchovies and coarsely chop. Add to tomatoes with garlic, olive oil, parsley, salt and pepper and mix well. Using a long sharp knife, thinly slice tuna. Arrange tuna slices on serving plates with salsa and serve.

Makes 6 servings.

SPICY JUMBO SHRIMP

2 garlic cloves, crushed
1 small bunch cilantro, finely chopped
Juice of 2 limes
1 fresh red chile, cored, seeded and finely chopped
1/3 cup sunflower oil
24 raw jumbo shrimp
GUACAMOLE:
1 garlic clove, crushed
4 tomatoes, peeled and finely chopped
1 fresh green chile, cored, seeded and finely
  chopped
Juice of 1 lime
2 tablespoons chopped fresh cilantro
Salt and freshly ground pepper
1 large ripe avocado

In a shallow nonmetallic dish, mix together garlic, cilantro, lime juice, chile and sunflower oil. Add shrimp and mix well. Cover and refrigerate 1 or 2 hours, turning occasionally. To make guacamole, put garlic, tomatoes, chile, lime juice, cilantro, salt and pepper into a bowl and mix well. Halve avocado lengthwise and remove pit. Using a teaspoon, scoop out flesh, taking care to scrape away dark green flesh closest to skin. Mash into tomato mixture.

Preheat broiler. Remove shrimp from marinade and arrange on broiler rack. Broil 2 or 3 minutes on each side, basting with marinade. Serve with guacamole and tortilla chips.

Makes 6 servings.

Note: Don't prepare the guacamole more than 30 minutes in advance or the avocado will discolor.

OYSTERS MEXICANA

24 oysters in shells
2 tomatoes, peeled and finely diced
4 green onions, finely chopped
1 fresh red chile, cored, seeded and finely chopped
2 tablespoons chopped fresh parsley
Juice of 1 lemon
Seaweed, to garnish (optional)

Spread cracked ice on a large tray and place oysters on top, to keep chilled. To open oysters, wrap a towel around one hand. Hold oyster, flat side up, in the protected hand. Insert blade of an oyster knife, or a short, rigid knife, into hinge of oyster shell.

Push and twist knife until you can prize open the shell. Discard top shell, taking care not to lose any juice, and slide knife under oyster to detach it from lower shell. Embed each oyster in ice until ready to serve.

In a bowl, mix together tomatoes, green onions, chile and parsley. Spread cracked ice on serving plates and arrange oysters on top. Spoon a little of the tomato mixture over each oyster, then sprinkle over a little lemon juice. Garnish with seaweed, if using, and serve.

Makes 4 servings.

INDEX